Captain Sir James O'Grady JP, KCMG
Taken when he was Governor of Tasmania, 1924–1930

THE LIFE OF CAPTAIN SIR JAMES O'GRADY J.P., K.C.M.G

Andrew Dennis

DIANA GILES

Diana Giles

Published by

MELROSE BOOKS

An Imprint of Melrose Press Limited
St Thomas Place, Ely
Cambridgeshire
CB7 4GG, UK
www.melrosebooks.co.uk

FIRST EDITION

Cover designed by Melrose Books

**ISBN   978-1-912026-77-7 hardback
978-1-912026-78-4 paperback**

Printed and bound in Great Britain by:
Berforts South West Ltd
17 Burgess Road
Ivyhouse Lane
Hastings
East Sussex
TN35 4NR

*To my husband, Tony, without whom
this book would never have been published.*

"Short-sighted is the philosophy that counts on selfishness as the master motive of human action"

James O'Grady
(from a book of favourite quotations published by the
East Hunslet Ward Labour Party

CONTENTS

LIST OF ILLUSTRATIONS

FOREWORD AND ACKNOWLEDGEMENTS

In this book, I have wanted to make a record of the entire life of my grandfather, James O'Grady. From my studies and researches, I have found him to be one of the most remarkable men of his time.

There are many brief records of his life and achievements and I have quoted extensively from them. The O'Grady family archives have formed the basis for the story; after that, the National Archives at Kew and the Royal Archives at Windsor Castle. I am most grateful to HM the Queen whose archivist, Miss Pamela Clark, and colleagues extended a warm welcome and made available to me all the relevant papers in their collection.

The librarians at Haywards Heath Library have been endlessly helpful and obtained for me the news cutting "leaked report" of the proposed appointment of the Ambassador to Russia.

The librarian at Crawley helped us to identify some of the old banknotes in the wallet which O'Grady took with him on his Famine Relief Mission.

Michael Whatley, the husband of Terence's daughter, Sheila O'Grady, set the scene by researching the O'Grady family tree.

My aunt, Nell (Ellen) O'Grady, became custodian of the family archive[1] because she cared for both her parents at the end of their lives. She handed the collection (as it was then) over to me when she found I had been researching the Russian episodes. Since then, many more papers have come to light with the death of other members of the family.

Molly's (Mary O'Grady) daughter, Mary Cameron, who spent two years of her early childhood in Tasmania with her grandfather, took a history degree in her seventies and did much research on his life and work.

---

1 Unfortunately, Nell allowed her (then) small daughter, Patricia, to deface so many of the letters by cutting out the signatures for her autograph album!

Joanna O'Grady's son, James Hill, found *Witnesses of the Revolution*.

Kitty (Catherine O'Grady) kept every letter and card from her father, and my mother, Norah O'Grady, talked to me all through her life of her father's career.

Thanks must also go to the younger generation – to Margaret's grandson, Simon Lincoln, and his wife Kim who rescued the letters from Litvinov which they found in a plastic shopping bag in an eave's cupboard when they cleared cousin Patricia's house after her death.

PART I

Forbears and Early Life

James O'Grady was described in *The Times* obituary as the most romantic of Labour Members of Parliament and, indeed, he was a romantic figure.

He was born in Bristol on 6th May, 1866, the youngest child of John O'Grady and Margaret Keiley. All his forbears were born in Ireland with the exception of his mother, born in Bristol of Irish-born parents.

Presumably, the two families, O'Grady and Keiley, left Ireland to escape the Great Famine of the first half of the 19th century.

They settled in the harbour area of Bristol in what was then a large Irish Catholic community, no doubt a lively and convivial scene despite the poverty and, of course, dominated by the Roman Catholic Church.

John and Margaret were married at St. Joseph's RC Church which later became St. Mary's on the Quay. Irish immigrants were not popular at the time, which is probably why the name was given as Grady at the marriage. All their children were baptized there.

James was educated at St. Mary's school in St. Augustine's Back, just across the water from Broad Quay (*see* Fig 1) where they all lived. St. Mary's school was governed by the Church of St. Mary's on the Quay, at that time a Jesuit Church. James would, therefore, have received his religious education from Jesuit priests and have been exposed to their preaching at the daily Assembly.

It has been suggested that his gift of oratory may have developed from this early influence.

We do not know from what age James attended the school, but he left at the age of 10 (or 12?) years to work in a mineral water factory, said to have been located in a cellar.

He had several other jobs before being apprenticed, on 6th December 1881, to the Chair and Coach Frame Maker, Edward William Harsop. (*see* page 3 for copy of the Indenture).

1

It is interesting to note the addresses of the witness to the Indenture, one from James Beecroft of 59 Queen Square. According to my mother, her grandparents, i.e., John and Margaret, lived in Queen Square when she was a child in the 1890s. The grandchildren were allowed to visit only two at a time. No doubt, by then, the elegant 18th century houses were in decline and were let out as rooms and apartments. They have now all been restored (*see* Fig 2).

On completion of his apprenticeship, James married Louise James (*see* Fig 3) in the Roman Catholic Church of the Holy Cross, Victoria Street, Bedminster on 30th July, 1887. James was 21 and Louise just 19. We are told they were childhood friends. Louise's maternal grandparents, James Connelly and Catherine Johnstone (b. 1794 and 1801 respectively) were born in Ireland, so no doubt the family was part of the Irish community in Bristol.

Louise was beautiful and intelligent. Cousin Joan tells us she was a teacher before her marriage which would probably have meant, then, a star pupil invited to stay on and teach the younger children at her school.

Louise was a great help to James in the self-education which he continued to the end of his life – witness the lists of words and their meanings found in his papers.

James wrote very good letters in a fine hand. He was exceptionally well read; no doubt the foundation for this was laid in his school days.

Cultural life in Bristol was rich and varied and, it would seem, enjoyed by all classes depending on their means. We know, for example, that James' sister, Mary (Polly), was a great opera fan and the contralto, Dame Clara Butt, was known by the family.

After his marriage, due to shortage of work, James was obliged to become a journeyman, i.e., a worker travelling in search of employment. This lasted for three years. We do not know how much time they were able to spend together, nor whether they had a home of their own, or whether Louise perhaps stayed with her parents.

In the course of his travels, James came into contact with the socialist ideas that were being discussed in the industrial centres and he began to take an interest in Trade Unionism and local politics.

Thus began the political career of James O'Grady.

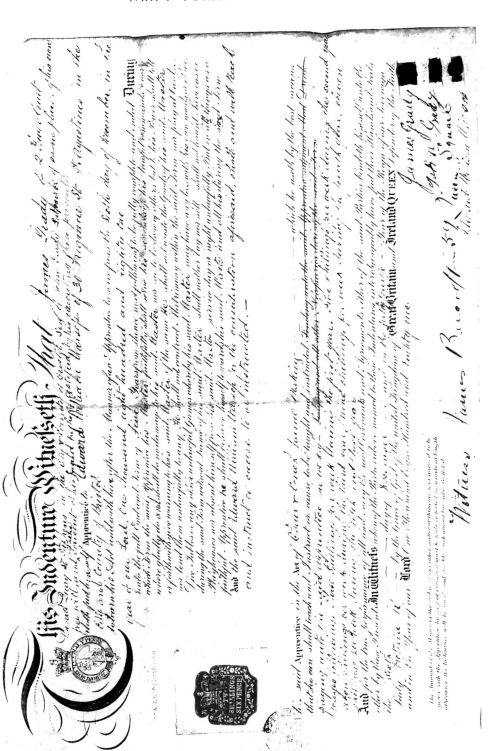

Fig 1 *Broad Quay, Bristol, courtesy Bristol Museums and Art Gallery*

Fig 2 *Queen Square. Watercolour by T.L. Rowbottom,*
Braikenridge Bequest, *1909. M 2206.*

Fig 3 *Louise (O'Grady archives)*   Fig 4 *Captain James O'Grady*
(photograph C. Vandyke Ltd)

Fig 5 *The Parliamentary Labour Party, Westminster 1906 (O'Grady second on the right). Copyright Photography, Barratt & Salisbury Court, Fleet St, EC*

PART II

POLITICAL LIFE

In 1890, O'Grady returned to Bristol from his working travels.

The city was then a hive of political activity. Hyndeman and his fellow Marxists were preaching revolution for which the workers seemed to have little inclination. Although he had already studied the work of Marx and Engels, O'Grady preferred the happier teachings of Carlisle, Morris and Ruskin and of Robert Blatchford, founder of the *Clarion* newspaper.

O'Grady made his first public speech in 1892, in support of the Bristol dockers who were on strike. He was already a fluent speaker with a soft Irish brogue; his evident sincerity drew audiences and he became a popular figure in the local labour movement, serving as President of the Bristol Trades Council.

He became a city councillor in 1896: records of their meetings show that he brought to his work in that sphere the common sense which was his hallmark. Education was always one of his greatest interests and, at that time, he helped create scholarships for promising schoolchildren.

During this period, Louise gave birth to their first five children – daughters Catherine (Kitty), Norah, Mary (Molly) and Ellen (Nell), and their first son, Edward. We can imagine the joy at the birth of a son. However, at the age of only 18 months, Edward died of convulsions. Norah recalled her parents' anguish; her father paced the floor all night with his dead son in his arms.

In 1898, O'Grady became president of the Trades Union Congress, which met in the Colston Hall in Bristol. It was said, afterwards, that his fiery presidential address was the cause of the fire which broke out in the building that night! His speech included an attack on child labour and a proposal that the trade unions should have their own independent political party.

In 1899, the TUC established the Labour Representative Committee.

Shortly after, O'Grady became the national organiser for his own union, the Furnishing Trades Association. This necessitated moving to London where he lived, in Camden, with his family and where his second son, James, and his fifth daughter, Eileen, were born

During this time, he attended the first meeting, in 1903, of the Labour Representative Committee.

However, the family did not thrive in Camden and they returned to Bristol.

In 190?, a dispute in the furnishing trade took him to Leeds (where the Trades Council had been the first to affiliate to the Labour Representative Committee). The local paper, *The Weekly Citizen*, later described his relations with the employers as "stormy". Did this perhaps attract the local Labour Party to him? At the time, the East Leeds Labour Party were looking for a parliamentary candidate. He was adopted and elected in 1906, beating the Conservative opponent by 2091 votes.

Thus began his 18 years of service as MP to the City of Leeds, first to East Leeds and later to South.

The family moved to London once again, but this time O'Grady consulted a doctor friend as to where they should live – either Hampstead Heath or Clapham Common was the advice and as the latter had the benefit of an all-night tram service to Westminster, Clapham it was. For the first 15 years or so, the family lived in rented houses in one or other of the streets leading to the west-side of the common.

We do not know how much Louise was involved in her husband's political activities. She must always have been fully involved with her ever growing family and, so far as we know, there are no photographs of her with James at any of the political functions. One or other of his older daughters sometimes went with him on his electioneering campaigns.

Clapham was then a convivial place with a large Irish Catholic community and many interesting residents – actors, musicians, members of the Royal Households. This no doubt was due to the proximity of Westminster and the West End.

O'Grady entered parliament in 1906 with 28 other Labour members.

In his maiden speech, he spoke in favour of Home Rule for Ireland, unsurprisingly. Hansard records that "he wanted, as an Irishman, to refer to the constant taunt that only one portion of Ireland was loyal. His answer to this was to be found in the record of Irishmen who had come from the South and West and who had died to maintain the prestige of the British nation. "If they wished to get rid of all this bitterness upon Irish questions it would be well to cut out the religious controversy, and look at the subject from a broader point of view". The latter was the keynote to his approach to any problem.

The plight of the miners (so well described by Catherine Bailey in her book *Black Diamonds*) was something O'Grady sought to alleviate all his time in Parliament.

He also concerned himself with the Indian question. He described himself as a Labour Imperialist, but was critical of government handling of Indian affairs, viz. (Hansard)

Outrages by soldiers

Mr. O'Grady I beg to ask the Secretary of State for India whether his attention has been drawn to a case in which two soldiers on the road to Simla demanded some soda water from a native and that they were duly supplied with what they wanted, but that when payment was demanded one of the soldiers raised his rifle and shot the native in the chest, the bullet passing out his back; and whether, having regard to the frequency of these incidents in India, this case being the fifth of its kind during the present year, he will address the Government of India with a view to taking stringent measures to prevent their recurrence.

Mr. Lea May I be permitted, Sir, before the Question is answered, to enter a protest against the wording of the Question.

Mr. Speaker The hon. Member may ask a Question.

Mr. Lea May I ask the right hon. Gentleman whether, considering that there are 80,000 white soldiers in India, even if it be true that there have been five cases of shooting during the year, he thinks that justifies putting the Question in this way.

Mr. Morley I rather sympathise with what has fallen from the hon. Gentleman behind me. I have no information as to the case stated in the Question but if the hon. Member who put the Question will give me the necessary information, I will make inquiries.

Mr. O'Grady Am I to understand that the government are in sympathy with the shooting of black people in this way.

Mr. Morley I cannot think that that is a Question I can be expected to answer.

Mr. O'Grady Is it the fact that four cases have already been proved to the satisfaction of the Secretary of State for India.

Sir Horton There is a report of this case in the Indian newspapers by this Mail.

Mr. Morley Need I say that if these cases are accurately reported, and some, I am afraid, have been accurately reported, I will at once give them my most prompt and earnest attention. Nobody has a more complete detestation of such acts than I have.

Mr. O'Grady The effect of the right hon. Gentleman's Answer has been to indicate some kind of approval of this procedure. That is the effect of the right hon. Gentleman's Answer. It bore that interpretation.

This is interesting to remember today (autumn 2013) when we learn of the conviction for murder by a Marine of an Afghan wounded insurgent, and how this has been handled by the establishment.

The record of Hansard for the years 1906, when O'Grady entered parliament, to 1908 shows us the breadth of his interest in the government of the country. Also, on Thursday 7th December, 1916, at noon, a deputation of Labour representatives waited on the new Prime Minister (Lloyd George) with a view to hearing what he had to say before they consented to support the government. It was obvious from the proceedings that the deputation contained members, particularly Sidney Webb, who did not desire the Labour Party to join in and support the government. Subsequently, in fact, the Labour Party split into two groups, the smaller one pacifist and the larger patriotic.

Undoubtedly, O'Grady will have been in the larger, patriotic group.

The first quarter of the 20th century were fruitful years for O'Grady. We are told by one of his successors in the constituency, Hilary Benn, that he was a good MP, much appreciated by his constituents; and by the *Dictionary of Labour Biography* that:

> He was loyal to his country when war broke out and that he subsequently did much to promote the war efforts of the government.

O'Grady's own record of his public service follows, with some of the letters inviting him to these endeavours:

Record of public Service
James O'Grady K.C.M.G.

1. Member of Bristol Town Council 1898
2. Member of Parliament continuous 1906–24
   Member of standing Committees of House of Commons
   Member of numerous select Committees set up by government to enquire into social evils and abuses with a view to legislation
3. Justice of Peace London since 1908
4. At beginning of great war helped to raise men, money and expedite output of munitions by addressing public meetings and men in factories

5. Member of Central Tribunal – the final Court of Appeal dealing with Conscientious Objectors and claims for exemption from military service
6. Engaged in many unofficial missions during the war for the British Government
7. As a civilian at the suggestion of the British Government visited the French, Belgian, American and British armies in the various theatres of war
8. Together with Sir Harry Britain was in charge of the American Civil Delegation on a tour of the Western Front, 1917 – in the main to visit the American troops. Appointed to the work by British Government
9. Appointed by Government as member of joint French and British Members of Parliament to visit Russia, 1917, with the purpose of keeping Russians loyal allies after the revolution, Feb 1917 (*see* Part IV)
10. Captain in army, 1918, and allocated for special services – particularly in Ireland, on voluntary recruiting
11. Appointed by Lord Curzon, Secretary of State for Foreign Affairs, to meet representative of Soviet Government in Copenhagen, 1920, to arrange exchange of the prisoners of war and to arrange repatriation of British nationals at the time resident in Russia. Agreement reached and document published as Command Paper (*see* Part IV)
12. Governor of Tasmania, Australia, 1924–30
13. Governor and C. in C. of the Falkland Islands and its Dependencies, 1931

In all, a summary of 35 years of public service.

National Service Department.

All Communications to be
addressed to
THE SECRETARY,
quoting this reference:—

WAA/DG   T/L

Telephone: Victoria 9300.
Telegrams: "NATSERVICE."

ROOM.............., ST. ERMINS,

WESTMINSTER, S.W.

7th March, 1917.

Dear Sir,

The burden of providing labour for occupations of primary importance has been placed upon the National Service Department. As Director General of this Department, I know how difficult it is to avoid pressing unduly upon interests that are affected.

In order to safeguard, as far as possible, the vital interests of work people, I have decided to appoint a very small Labour Advisory Committee.

I know that there are already many claims upon your time, but in view of the importance of this matter to your own members, as well as to the general body of work people, I trust you will be able to accept the invitation to serve which I cordially extend.

Efforts will be made to epitomise the work of the Committee so as to avoid all unnecessary waste of time.

Yours faithfully,

DIRECTOR GENERAL.

James O'Grady Esq., J.P., M.P.;
74, Manchuria Road,
Clapham Common, S.W.

7th August, 1918.

Dear Captain O'Grady,

Many thanks for your letter of the 5th instant.

I congratulate you on getting into khaki, and still more that you are off to Ireland determined to do your best to make voluntary recruiting in that country a success.

I have informed the King of your mission, and needless to say His Majesty is delighted to hear of this good news and wishes you all success.

Yours sincerely
Stamfordham

Captain James O'Grady, M.P.,
    National Federation of
            General Workers,
        Granville House,
            Arundel Street,
                Strand,
                    LONDON, W.C.2.

Home Office,
Whitehall,
S.W.1.

21st February, 1919.

Dear Captain O'Grady

I have decided to appoint a Committee, consisting of
Members of both Houses of Parliament, to consider and report
whether any and what changes should be made in the method of
recruiting for, the conditions of service of, and the rates
of pay, pensions and allowances of the Police Forces of England,
Wales and Scotland; and I should be very glad if you would
consent to be a member of the Committee.

It is in my opinion very desirable that the Committee
should report at as early a date as possible, and for that
reason should meet frequently. While therefore the work of the
Committee is likely to be heavy, I hope that it will not be of
long duration.

The subject which the Committee will have to consider is
one of the greatest importance, and I should much value the
assistance you could give to me and to the Government by consenting
to serve on the Committee.

As I am most anxious to announce the appointment and con-
stitution of the Committee immediately, I should be grateful if
you would reply to this letter at your earliest convenience.

Yrs Sincerely

Edward Short

James O'Grady, Esq., M.P.

DISARMAMENT CONFERENCE

O'Grady attended a Disarmament Conference in Amsterdam in November 1921, as reported in the following letter to Lord Curzon from Mr. Knatchbull Hugesson of the British Legation in the Hague:

BRITISH LEGATION,
THE HAGUE.
November 26th, 1921

My Lord:-

With reference to Sir Ronald Graham's despatch No.646 of October 26th last I have the honour to report that according to "Het Volk" of November 18th a disarmament conference was held on the 15th and 16th November at Amsterdam and was attended by representatives of the International Federations of Transport Workers, Miners and Metal Workers. It was decided to form a provisional committee to carry on anti-militarist propaganda and action pending the International Congress to be held at Rome in April 1922. This committee is to be composed of the members of the Bureau of the International Federation of Trades Unions, Robert Williams for the Transport Workers, Frank Hodges for the Miners and C. Ilg for the Metal Workers.

James O'Grady, appointed by the International Federation of Trades Unions as their general representative at Petrograd for the alleviation of distress in Russia, was present at the meeting of the 16th November.

Three resolutions were passed:-

(1) An appeal to the working classes of all countries to devote all their attention and energy to fighting capitalism and militarism which is inseparable from capitalism, and to stop work in the event of war.

(2) The Conference representing and speaking on behalf of 24,000,000 organised workmen, made a special appeal to women to fight side by side with workmen in order to prevent war, and

(3) A decision to form the above-mentioned provisional committee.

I have the honour to be, with the highest respect,

My Lord,
Your Lordship's most obedient,
humble Servant

PART III

FAMILY LIFE

James and Louise's eighth child was born in Bristol in 1905 – Margaret. As eldest unmarried daughter at the time, she accompanied her father to Tasmania.

The two youngest children were born in Clapham, Terence and Joanna, and it was about this time that Louise developed the rhodent ulcer which went untreated and caused so much suffering for her and grief for the family.

It would seem that for James and Louise theirs was a great love affair and, so far as we know during their time together, James never succumbed to the many temptations which come to men of power. Louise was well aware of them and perhaps the number of children born to them is evidence of her reluctance ever to refuse him.

One of the temptations was undoubtedly the Countess of Warwick. She had converted to Socialism and was wont to invite the Labour MPs to her home for the occasional weekend.

There is no record of James ever attending. He was well aware of her predatory sexual inclinations. It was not many years since the scandal of the "My darling Daisie" letters from Edward Prince of Wales which had driven the Princess of Wales to extend her annual summer holiday with her family in Denmark. Only the earnest entreaties of Queen Victoria had persuaded her to return.

However, there must have been some contact between the Countess and James, because his daughter, Catherine, remembered a coach, bearing the Warwick Arms, occasionally delivering a brace or two of pheasant to the O'Grady home.

So much of James' time was, of course, spent away from home so Louise was often without his support during her 20 years of child bearing and rearing.

"TE EXTRA"

ONE PENNY.

NEWS."

"GRAND LADY" AT EIGHTEEN.

THE KING'S COMPLIMENT TO MISS O'GRADY.

Miss Margaret O'Grady has always had an ambition—to be a mannequin—and she has the ideal figure for it. But now, at the age of 18, she is to be the "Grand Lady" of Government House, Hobart, Tasmania.

Her father, Mr. James O'Grady, the Labour leader, is the newly-appointed representative of the King there, and so for the time Miss Margaret's dreams must yield to realities.

Her journey to Tasmania will take her out of England for the first time. She has lived all her life at Clapham.

SHINGLED.

She has a plentiful share of Irish good looks, is just over 5ft. 6in. tall, and has beautiful hair—shingled.

When she was presented to the King at a Royal garden party the King remarked to her father: "Very fine girl, Mr. O'Grady."

At present Miss Margaret is helping to run the Clapham house—her mother is an invalid—and she declares that she loves cooking as well as dancing, and finds housekeeping "lots of fun."

She is also pondering over exciting essentials—for a Government House hostess—such as frocks and servants.

"One of my sisters is coming over from Paris to help me choose my clothes," she told me to-day (writes an Evening News woman representative). "She is married to an artist and knows all about dress."

I recall James was a very loving father and grandfather and he particularly appreciated his sons-in-law, especially David Ballantine (Catherine's husband), with whom he corresponded frequently; and Norah's husband, Sydney Martin, whom he called the long'un – he was 6'4". Perhaps this was because he had only two surviving sons – both wayward in their youth. The eldest, Jim, when called to account, said he was intending to go and join the South African Mounted Police. Jim was somewhat dismayed to find himself on the next boat to Cape Town!

(Young Jim subsequently became a rubber planter in Malaya, was taken prisoner by the Japanese in Singapore in February 1942, put into Changi Jail and then taken to work on the Burma railway, which he survived.)

James was particularly proud of his daughters. Winston Churchill complimented him on his beautiful girls and, as reported in the newspaper (*see* left) King George V thought Margaret "a very fine girl".

All the children received a good education and they were

all taught to play a musical instrument. On Sunday evenings, a family concert was held in which, in later years, the sons-in-law joined.

Despite Louise's affliction, it was a happy, lively household, always with many friends visiting and occasionally priests and nuns.

Both Louise and James were brought up in the Roman Catholic Faith and held strongly to it all their lives.

James missed his family terribly when he was away.

It was not possible for Louise to go with him to Tasmania. She had a special mask made and went to show it to her daughter, Catherine, but she could not bear the pain of it against her face.

James did not want to go without her, but she was insistent – in her view, it was the pinnacle of his career.

Before he left, James bought two neighbouring houses in Cavendish Road, where they lived, divided them into flats and installed in them his remaining daughters and their families so that Louise was surrounded by her family during his absence. Many of his 18 grandchildren were brought up together there and have remained close for the rest of their lives, which has been a great blessing. As I write, there are seven surviving grandchildren. (Diana Giles, New Year, 2017.)

PART IV

RUSSIA

PROLOGUE

In the early winter of 1919, there was much activity in the Gulf of Finland, most of it covert. In Petrograd, the Bolsheviks were struggling to retain their hold on Russia against counter revolution. There were many spies in the city, including Paul Dukes. A CMB captained by Augustus Agar VC, was in the Gulf on a mission to rescue him, but Lt. Bremner and other members of the crew had been captured during a skirmish and were now in prison in Petrograd.

With many others, Captain Agar and his remaining crew were anxiously awaiting the outcome of negotiations taking place in Copenhagen between Maxim Litvinov, then Soviet Foreign Minister, and the Labour MP, James O'Grady, who had been appointed by the British Foreign Secretary, Early Curzon, to represent the British government.

Maxim Litvinov was, at that time, persona non grata in Denmark due to his subversive activities in Scandinavia, and the Danish government had been reluctant to host the talks.

Their fears were well founded. We learn from Andrew Boyle in his book *Climate of Treason* (pages 31–34) that Litvinov was passing valuable jewellery (in a tobacco pouch) to Francis Meynell, one of the disaffected youth who had come to Copenhagen to make contact with him.

All this right under the nose of O'Grady.

.

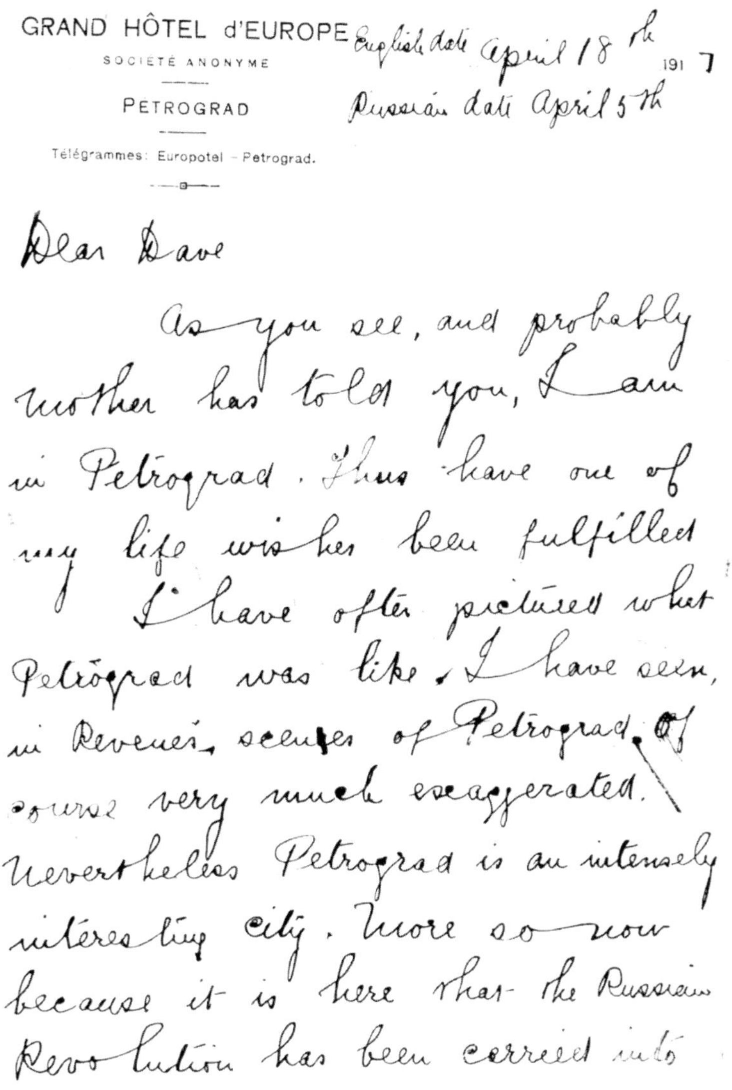

GRAND HÔTEL d'EUROPE *English date* April 18 th 191 7
SOCIETÉ ANONYME

Russian date April 5 th

PETROGRAD

Télégrammes: Europotel – Petrograd.

Dear Dave

As you see, and probably
mother has told you, I am
in Petrograd. Thus have one of
my life wishes been fulfilled
I have often pictured what
Petrograd was like. I have seen,
in Revenes, scenes of Petrograd. Of
course very much exaggerated.
Nevertheless Petrograd is an intensely
interesting city. More so now
because it is here that the Russian
Revolution has been carried into

Fig 1 *O'Grady's letter to his son-in-law (O'Grady archives)*
See text for full letter.

23

Dear Dave

As you see, and probably mother has told you, I am in Petrograd thus have one of my life wishes been fulfilled.

I have often pictured what Petrograd was like. I have seen the review scenes of Petrograd, of course very much exaggerated. Nevertheless Petrograd is an intensely interesting city. More so now because it is here that the Russian Revolution has been carried into effect. Let it be said at once that it was a soldier's revolution, not civilian. Two famous Russian Regiments were responsible for its success. First the famous Preobrazhensky Regiment which was raised by one of the old Czars from the Moscow district. They are that regiment of giants with the peculiar "mitre" headdress that you have seen, no doubt, in the illustrated papers. This regiment were instructed to leave barracks and fire on the crowd. This they point-blank refused to do. That was the first sensation. Then the Cossacks, a magnificent body of horses in picturesque uniform all fairly well-to-do men in peace times; were ordered to charge the crowd. They simply walked their horses through the people. The latter, astonished at this demeanour on the part of the Cossacks, wildly cheered. The Gendarmes and Police seeing this charged the crowd cutting right and left. Then the Cossacks started on the Gendarmes and Police and chased them through the streets. "Glory Hallelujah". The Gendarmes and Police afterwards shed their uniforms and got into civilian clothes. At the moment the order and good conduct of the city is in the hands of the soldiers. The city itself is, as I say, intensely interesting. There are great wide streets and open spaces. Magnificent churches of peculiar architecture. The noble river "Neva" about half as wide again as the Thames at Westminster, running through the city. When we arrived here the thaw had set in and the ice on the river was breaking. For 6 months of the year Petrograd is under snow and ice. But it must be a charming city in the summer especially in peace time. The cost of living in Russia is atrociously high. I make it to be at least 200 per cent above the normal. The cost of a "droshky" – an ordinary horse cab for the shorter of drives is such as only to tempt the very well-to-do folks to take it on. I have written nothing of politics as it is not wise at the moment, even in "free" Russia. Love and kisses to Kitty and the kiddies. Good luck and wishes

Yours lovingly Dad

Fig 2 *The Grand Hotel d'Europe, St. Petersburg (Petrograd) in 2001.*
Courtesy The Grand Hotel

Fig 3 *Will Thorne, O'Grady and Lt. Sanders with soldiers in the amphitheatre of the Duma. Photograph G. Boulla, Petrograd Nevsky Prospect 54*

Fig 4 *Members of the Delegation. Photograph G. Boulla, Petrograd Nevsky Prospect 54*

Fig 5 *A delegate addressing the crowd.*
Photograph G. Boulla, Petrograd Nevsky Prospect 54

Fig 6 *The Tauride Palace, home of the Duma. O'Grady Archives*

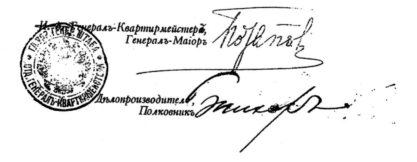

ГЛАВНОЕ УПРАВЛЕНІЕ
ГЕНЕРАЛЬНАГО ШТАБА.
ОТДѢЛЪ
Генералъ-Квартирмейстера.

Особое Дѣлопроизводство.

"15" Апрѣля 1917 г.
№ 2029
Петроградъ.

УДОСТОВѢРЕНІЕ.

Дано сіе отъ Главнаго Управленія Генеральнаго Штаба _Великобританскому_ _подданому г-ку О'Гради_ на свободный проѣздъ _въ Штабъ Сѣвернаго и За-_ _паднаго фронтовъ, съ просьбой_ _оказать возможное содѣйствіе._ Дѣйствительно до "15" Мая 1917 г., послѣ чего подлежитъ возвращенію въ Главное Управленіе Генеральнаго Штаба.

И. д. Генералъ-Квартирмейстера,
Генералъ-Маіоръ

Дѣлопроизводитель,
Полковникъ

Fig 7 *Safe passage pass for O'Grady to the Northern and Western Fronts.* *(O'Grady archives)*

Fig 8 *O'Grady's passport. (O'Grady archives)*

Fig 9 Temporary passport issued by British Ambassador, Sir George Buchanan, dated 14th May, 1917. (O'Grady archives)

CHAPTER 1

1917 REVOLUTION

In the spring of 1917, O'Grady was appointed by the War Cabinet[2] to join a joint British and French delegation to the Provisional Government in Petrograd to persuade that government to continue the war against Germany.

Revolution had broken out in February; the Tsar[3] was forced to abdicate on March 15th and the government of the country was in the hands of the social revolutionaries who formed the Provisional Government with, first, Prince Lvov at its head and, by April, Alexander Kerensky.

O'Grady described the February/March revolution in his letter dated 5th/18th April from the Grand Hotel d'Europe, where he was staying, to his son-in-law, David Ballantine (*see* Figs 1 and 2).

The other members of the British delegation were Will Thorne, Labour MP, and Lt. W. S. Sanders, Secretary of the Fabian Society, who was to act as secretary to the delegation; Messrs. Montet, Cachin and Lafont being the French members.

Presumably, they travelled to Petrograd by ship, a British warship, sailing through the Gulf of Finland, passing Kronstadt, the naval base and scene of the mutiny of 1905, then into Petrograd on the River Neva, mooring, perhaps, alongside some of the magnificent palaces before the Lieutenant Schmidt Bridge. The date was Friday April 13th.

We have O'Grady's passport with its many official stamps marking arrivals and departures (*see* Fig 8).

There are many contemporary reports of the mission; perhaps the mot interesting is the following report by the journalist Harold Williams, which appears in *Witnesses of the Revolution*, by Harvey Pitcher:

---

2 Appendix II War Cabinet Minutes
3 *See* notes on Chapter 1

On Friday, April 13th, a British Labour delegation, consist-ing of Messrs. Thorne, O'Grady and Sanders, arrived in Petrograd in company with three French socialist delegates and the veteran Russian socialist leader, Plekanov.[4] At three o'clock on Sunday, they all went to the main hall of the Duma where the conference was still in sessions. The amphitheatre, Harold Williams writes, 'which one had been accustomed to see occupied by the sober figures of Deputies, was filled with picturesque soldiers and workmen (*see* Fig 5), all intent on the new and serious business.

The entry of the delegates and Plekanov was the signal for cheering. Business was interrupted as Messrs. Plekanov, Thorne, O'Grady, Moutet and Cachin were led up to the Speaker's chair, and M. Chkeidze, President of the Soviet, said a few words of welcome. It was an amazing sight to see Mr. Thorne, with a big fur coat over his arm, standing amid the throng of Russian Socialists on the official tribune of the Duma. Mr. Cachin, the French delegate, made an impas-sioned speech to the audience, which did not understand a word, but responded to the thrilling inflections and dramatic gestures of the French orator. The cheering was still more lusty when his speech was translated by a member of the Russian Executive Committee.

Then Mr. O'Grady spoke. He began in a low voice, and I was afraid his speech would be less effective than that of the Frenchman's. But in two minutes, he had raised his voice to Trafalgar Square dimensions, and the decorous Duma had never heard such a volume of thunderous sound as Mr. O'Grady poured forth on the uncomprehending soldiers and workmen. They were great impressed, and when the translator announced that Mr. O'Grady was chair-man of the National Federation of Trade Unions, there was

---

4 Georgi Valentinovich Plekanov, 1857–1918, known as the father of the Russian Revolution.

a tumult of applause, which was renewed again and again during the translation of the speech. Neither M. Cachin, nor Mr. O'Grady mentioned the war. They conveyed greetings from the Western Workers, and spoke glowingly of the liberative effect of the Russian Revolution on the world. Mr. Plekanov did speak of the war, and most definitely and emphatically, and his words were cheered to the echo.

Then, on the spot where only a few months ago I had heard Sturmer mumbling his lying assurances about loyalty to the Allies and war to victory, Mr. Plekanov seized Mr. O'Grady by one hand and M. Moutet by the other, and raising them on high, presented the wildly cheering throng a real and thrilling symbol of allied democracy. "It was admirable, it was moving" said M. Cachin, as we walked out.

Ransome devotes only half a dozen lines to this event; compared to the tremendous receptions given to Breshko-Breshkovskaya and Plekanov, the arrival of the allied delegates "naturally uncaused (sic) very great excitement". Phillips Price was present when the delegates visited Moscow and met a deputation from the local Soviet to discuss the revolutionaries' peace programme. The British position was uncompromising.

No peace, they said, could be obtained by such means. Only the complete military defeat and crushing of Germany for many years to come would bring peace in the world. "But even if that were the best tactics to adopt for destroying Prussian militarism, which is as much our enemy as it is yours" said one of the Russians, "is that any reason why we should not renounce the old annexationist plans of the Tsar's late regime and publish the secret treaties? The Tsar made us fight for Constantinople, which is not Russian, and never was". One of the British delegates thereupon jovially burst out: "If you don't want Constantinople, then, damn it, we'll take it!" I remember a long silence after this remark, then handshaking and the withdrawal of the deputation.

At one stage, the delegates were denounced as government agents, which, in a sense, they were. However, the veteran socialist, Hyndeman, telegraphed to Kerensky a full record of their public work, which restored confidence in them as true representatives of the Labour Party.

The report which the British delegation submitted to the War Cabinet on their return home obviously gives the best account of their mission (Appendix II).

The delegates returned to London on May 25th, via Stockholm, where they held discussions with Branting, Huysman and others on the proposed separate conferences between the various socialist majorities and minorities.

In an interview on his return, O'Grady declared that what Russia most needed was the confidence, sympathy and support of the Allied peoples. He uttered a grave warning against German propaganda in Russia, largely anti-British, which was being conducted with a lavish expenditure of money, while our Government was doing nothing.

Following their mission, it was decided that an opportunity should be given for the delegates to be interviewed briefly by the War Cabinet (Minutes of the War Cabinet, July 2nd 1917). In July, O'Grady was called to the palace to be received by the king. (*See* page 35.)

The mission would appear to have succeeded since the Provisional Government made no attempt to seek a separate peace treaty with the Germans. Bruce Lockhart, in his Memoirs of a British Agent lays, on the mission, some of the blame for the success of the October revolution which brought the Bolsheviks to power, since, he says, continuation of the war further weakened the already overstretched resources of the Russians and made the Provisional Government unpopular.

Following the October revolution, the Bolsheviks sued for a separate peace with the Germans which took Russia out of the war in March 1918 by the Treaty of Brest Litovsk.

LETTER FROM LORD STAMFORDHAM

BUCKINGHAM PALACE

16th.June 1917.

Dear Mr O'Grady,

      The King will receive you here at 11 a.m. on Tuesday next (19th.inst). Please let me know that this day and hour will be convenient for you.

                    Yours very truly,

                    Stamfordham

James O'Grady Esq:
        M.P.

Notes to Part IV, Chapter 1

On the evening of 15th March 1917, seated alone in his private railway compartment, Nicholas abdicated.

....

The Tsar came home to find he was to be a prisoner in one of his own palaces. With Alexandra and the children and a tiny remnant of his retinue, Nicholas was confined, through the spring and summer of 1917, in the fairytale palace of Tsarskoe Selo a few miles south of St. Petersburg. The danger to the family was real. In the Petrograd Soviet – the Council of revolutionary workers and soldiers – there was talk of vengeance for generations of oppression. The extremists were calling for Romanov blood. But the new Minister of Justice, Alexander Kerensky, rejected such talk, exclaiming "I will not be the Marat of the Russian Revolution. The Russian Revolution does not take vengeance".

While Kerensky lasted the Romanovs were safe.

(The File on the Tsar – Anthony Summers and Tom Mangold)

From *A Lifelong Passion* by Andrei Maylunas & Sergei Miromenko

Lord Stamfordham to A. J. Balfour – 21 March – Buckingham Palace
My dear Balfour,
I have received and laid before the King your letter of the 2nd. inst. respecting the proposal that the Emperor Nicholas and his family should come to England.
As His Majesty's Ministers are still anxious that the King should adhere to the original invitation sent on their advice His Majesty must regard the matter as settled, unless the Russian Government should come to any fresh decision on the subject.
Yours very truly, Stamfordham

Maurice Paléologue, Memoirs – 21 March
At five o'clock I went to see the Grand Duke Nikolai Mikhailovich in his palace, which is full of Napoleonic relics. It is the first time I have had the chance of a talk with him since the revolution.
He affected an optimism to which silence was my only reply. But he certainly carried it no further than the occasion warranted and, to prevent me thinking that he was entirely hoodwinked by the course of events, he concluded with this cautious reservation:
'As long as sensible and patriotic men like Prince Lvov, Milyukov and Guchkov are at the head of the government, I shall be hopeful enough. If they fall, we are in for a leap into the unknown.'
'In the first chapter of Genesis, that "unknown" is given a specific name.'
'Really! What?'
'The *Tohu-bohu*, which means "chaos".'

22 March The Minister of Justice, Kerensky, yesterday paid a visit to Tsarskoe Selo to see for himself the arrangements made for guarding the ex-sovereigns. He found everything in order.
Count Benckendorff, Grand Marshal of the Court; Prince Dolgorukov, Marshal of the Court; Madame Naryschkin, Mistress of the Robes; Mlles. Buxhoeveden and Hendrikov,[13] Maids of Honour, and the Tsarevich's tutor, Gilliard, are sharing their monarch's captivity. Madame Vyrubova, who was also residing in the Alexander Palace, has been forcibly removed and confined in the Fortress of SS. Peter and Paul – in the famous Trubetskoi bastion.
Kerensky had a talk with the Emperor. In particular he asked him whether it were true, as the German papers have reported, that William II had frequently advised him to adopt a more liberal policy.
But the Empress was as frigid as she could be.
Madame Vyrubova's departure has not affected her, at any rate in the way that might have been expected. After all her passionate and jealous attachment to her, she has suddenly made her responsible for all the evils which have overtaken the Russian imperial family.

XENÍA TO NICKY – 23 MARCH – ST PETERSBURG
I have been sitting here in the hope that they would let me through to you, as my

---
[13] A. Hendrikov. In 1918 she was arrested in Ekaterinburg and shot.

one wish was to see you. Now it has become clear it isn't feasible, and I leave for the Crimea on the 25th.

You will understand how painful and sad it is for me, but what can I do, I have to give up. I have been with you heart and soul during the dear children's illness, afraid from afar, without news, suffering as I suffer now for your sufferings, living everything with you. Today Mama, Sandro and Olga and her husband are going to the Crimea. They will be staying with us.

It will be very painful for poor Mama to return there, but at least we will all be together, and that is a real comfort at such a time! It is so sad that you cannot come and join us! I want to believe that everything will end well for Russia and the war will be brought to a victorious end.

My heart bleeds for you, for our country, for everything. But the God of the Russian land is great, and we have to believe and pray and put our faith in God's mercy. Please God we shall meet again in better circumstances – but where, when and how?

Nicky, Diary – 23 March – Tsarskoe Selo
I looked through my books and things, and started to put aside everything that I want to take with me, if we have to go to England.

25 March, The Annunciation   We spent this feast day in unbelievable conditions – under arrest in our own house and without the slightest possibility of communicating either with Mama or our relatives!

Lord Stamfordham to A. J. Balfour – 24 March – Windsor Castle
My dear Balfour,

Every day the King is becoming more concerned about the question of the Emperor and Empress of Russia coming to this country.

His Majesty receives letters from people in all classes of life, known or unknown to him, saying how much the matter is being discussed, not only in Clubs but by working men, and that Labour Members in the House of Commons are expressing adverse opinions to the proposal.

As you know from the first the King has thought the presence of the Imperial Family (especially of the Empress) in this country would raise all sorts of difficulties, and I feel sure that you appreciate how awkward it will be for our Royal Family who are closely connected both with the Emperor and Empress.

You probably also are aware that the subject has become more or less public property, and that people are either assuming that it has been initiated by the King, or deprecating the very unfair position in which His Majesty will be placed if the arrangement is carried out.

The King desires me to ask you whether after consulting the Prime Minister, Sir George Buchanan should not be communicated with with a view to approaching the Russian Government to make some other plan for the future residence of Their Imperial Majesties?

Yours very truly, Stamfordham

CHAPTER II

THE AFTERMATH OF WAR

Exchange of prisoners and repatriation of civilians

In November 1919, O'Grady was appointed by the Foreign Secretary, Lord Curzon, Head of the British Delegation for the exchange of prisoners of war and civilian nationals, to meet, in Copenhagen, representatives of the Soviet government. Maxim Litvinov was the representative appointed by the Soviets.

The meetings took place at the HQ of the Danish Red Cross. The negotiations were difficult and protracted and we know that O'Grady returned home in December to spend Christmas with his family. (There are in the PRO Archives[5] some papers relating to the question of payment for his passage home!)

O'Grady's report, *see* Appendix III, dated July 5th, 1920, to Earl Curzon gives a graphic description of his negotiations with Litvinov and a detailed description of how the agreements reached were carried out. Litvinov was at this time *persona non grata* in Scandinavia due to his efforts to spread communism in those countries. Denmark was therefore reluctant to host the meeting. Litvinov had spent many years in England and had an English wife. He was always anxious to maintain good relations with the West. He was, in fact, a statesman and, had his political career prospered instead of Stalin's, the history of the 20th century might have been very different. As it was, it was amazing that he was not liquidated by Stalin.

In his book *Between the Revolution and the West*, Hugh Phillips quotes Litvinov recalling that early in their talks O'Grady said he might have trouble "finding a common language with the representative of a country that had exterminated its crowned head". Litvinov eyed

---

5 Now the National Archives

O'Grady and said that unless his memory failed him, he believed that the English had sent a king to the executioner's block. According to Litvinov, O'Grady quickly changed the subject and became lost in a cloud of cigar smoke!

Does his memory serve him correctly? Can we believe that a man chosen for his tact and patience would really have made such a remark in the opening stags of difficult negotiations?

In his book *The Story of ST25*, the SS agent, Paul Dukes, gives a horrifying account of life in Petrograd in 1919/20, very different from that given by Litvinov to O'Grady. The Bolsheviks were in constant fear of attack from counter revolutionaries and from the western powers, and no-one was safe from imprisonment or death.

We also learn, from many books written about this period, of the situation prevailing, at that time, in Russia and in the Baltic.

In *Baltic Episode* by Capt. Augustus Agar VC, we learn that, at the end of their gallant campaign, they were awaiting anxiously the conclusion of the O'Grady/Litvinov negotiations and the resulting repatriation of the captured survivors of those battles including Lt. Bremner mentioned in the report.

To quote from Capt. Agar:

> The negotiations dragged on for weeks, then months, and our men did not finally return until April, 1920, after spending six dreadful weeks with ordinary criminals in the Schpalernaya prison at Petrograd and five months in the notorious Androniev monastery at Moscow, which the Bolsheviks converted into a prison for white Russian counter-revolutionaries and prisoners of other nationalities including French and British who fell into their hands on various fronts.
>
> Our C.M.B. men were transferred there from Petrograd and suffered the most frightful privations. Describing their transfer, Giddy wrote: "During the three days journey from Petrograd to Moscow we were given no food, except at one station where soldiers brought us bread and weak tea. We

were desperate with hunger and at one stop where a farm cart drew up with potatoes and carrots, we grabbed handfuls and ate them raw much to our subsequent discomfort …

Eventually we arrived at Moscow where the whole trainload of prisoners were divided into two parties. The first went to the Cheka prison; the other, of which we formed part, were consigned to the Androniev Monastery on the outskirts of the city. We refused to march, as Bremner was incapable of walking, and after much heated discussion a cart was found for him.

Our party consisted mostly of Russians with as many women as men. We marched in column. Next to us, an old lady in a faded black satin dress hobbled along on high-heeled shoes, bent under the weight of a sack bulging with old belongings. When we relieved her of this she thanked us in fluent English. She was born a Princess.

Near us, too, marched a huge man in an old-fashioned frock coat, topped incongruously by a checked cap. He hailed us in American English and was very friendly, but the Princess told us to be careful as he was an *agent provocateur* amongst the prisoners … few dared to speak to anyone …

The monastery lies on the top of a small hill overlooking the city and is most impressive. We passed through the great gateway and halted inside the walls which enclosed a cemetery and were kept there for some time, until Napier, myself and the six ratings were taken to a separate building containing two large rooms. In the darkness it was some seconds before I realised the rooms were full of people. They were British soldiers.

We had heard there were British prisoners of war in Moscow, but to stumble on them like this was wonderful. Our depression vanished and our hunger as well, for, crowding around us to hear our story, they pressed on us precious food they had carefully hoarded for emergencies …

They were a mixed collection. Several officers captured in a White Russian mutiny at Inega. R.F.C. officers force landed in Odessa and Murmansk. Soldiers serving in regiments in North Russia and so on … We spent five months in this monastery. There was a large contingent of French, mainly business men, some Germans, a few Hungarians and Central Europeans. Conditions were appalling … our personal cleanliness sadly deteriorated and lice never left us until we left Russia. We washed under a pump in the yard until it froze …"

James O'Grady, c1919. (O'Grady archives)   *Maxim Litvnov from* Between the Revolution and the West by Hugh Phillips

O'Grady. M.P.

Will you please ask the Russians if
have my boy *written to* prisoner?
Yours respectfully
A. M. Tennant

£50 (Fifty Pounds) REWARD
(£5 Reward for information leading to his discovery)

To anyone who can find and bring home

Private **ALLAN JOHN TENNANT**
No. 510354, 13th Platoon, 'D' Company,
1st BATTALION LONDON SCOTTISH,
MISSING NOVEMBER 24th, 1917.
CAMBRAI BATTLE.

Near Bapaume-Cambrai Road, Tadpole Copse and Sugar Factory.
Variously reported as a Prisoner in Germany, and Wounded in British Hospital.

In his pocket would be a Brown Leather Chess Case.

Apply—

Mrs. TENNANT, HEATH VIEW, CRANFORD ROAD, HESTON, HOUNSLOW.

THOMASONS LTD., HOUNSLOW.

Fig 1 *Poster regarding Private Tennant. (O'Grady archives)*

43

Fig 2 *Earl Curzon.*
(Source unknown)

Fig 3 *HQ of the Danish Red Cross where*
the negotiations took place. By courtesy of
the Royal Library, Copenhagen, Depart-
ment of Maps, Prints and Photography

Mr. O'GRADY RETURNS.—Mr. J. O'Grady, M.P. (centre), after his arrival at Liverpool-street last night on his return from Copenhagen, where he
has been negotiating with M. Litvinoff, the Soviet emissary, in regard to the
exchange of prisoners. He states that an agreement has been signed.

Fig 4 *'Mr. O'Grady returns'. Newspaper report*

Hugh Phillips quotes that, at their parting, O'Grady asked Litvinov if his family had left England with the intention of returning with him to Russia. Litvinov replied in the affirmative. "For how long?" asked O'Grady. "For good," was Litvinov's reply. In September 1920, they sailed for Petrograd.

The emotive impact of the negotiations is perhaps demonstrated by the poster (*see* Fig 4) which was sent to O'Grady by a grieving anxious mother.

See also Appendix IV for the list of British prisoners given to J O'G and signed by Litvinov.

The negotiations were concluded in March 1920 and James returned to London and presented his report to the Foreign Secretary.

We do not know if Private Tennant was ever found. His name does not appear in Litvinov's list.

Footnote to Chapter II
In the context of this chapter, it is interesting to read the letter to King George V from his cousin "Ducky", Grand Duchess Cyril of Russia, born Princess Victoria Melitta of Edinburgh (*see* below).

Borgo, Finland
22nd July, 1919

My dear George,
Once more I have been asked by our leading men to give you a brief account of the present situation here. The kindness with which you answered my last letter enables me to do so.

We are fully aware of the reasons and difficulties the Allied Governments which are enducing them to withdraw from us their help at the most urgent moment. I see, however, that our representations have failed to give you the impression of the eminent danger such a course is creating, and of the European disaster it is conjuring up.

The present situation is as follows. Admiral Koltchak's retreat, caused by the want of ammunition etc., on which he had counted, has endangered General Denikin's successful advance. His right flank is exposed to the full forces which the Bolsheviks have been enabled to withdraw from the Eastern front and which they are now throwing against him and our North-Western Army. Should Denikin in consequence meet with the slightest defeat, even Finland, the last buffer between Northern Europe and bolshevism, must unavoidably succumb. To prevent such a contingency all our energies must be concentrated on the immediate taking and retaining of St. Petersburg by our North-Western Army. This can only be done with the help of Finland. All questions as to the participation of Finland in this undertaking have been clearly settled and accepted between General Judenitch and General Mannerheim.

General Mannerheim can march any moment if he receives from England the declaration that she will give Finland her full moral and material support without which he is not in a position to propose such a step to his Government, though he is backed by the whole of his country.

Finland is naturally too weak to support such an undertaking on her own. Therefore we ask that England should insist on Finland's immediate advance on Petersburg. Should, however, the English Government find it impossible for her own reasons to put this pressure on the present Finish Ministry she could achieve the same result by fully supporting General Judenitch and by supporting him with all necessary material support wherewith to supply Finland, as General Mannerheim and Judenitch are working in complete understanding, and mutual interests of their countries.

It is of the greatest urgency that the English Government should not lose a moment in doing this so that Petersburg should be taken in the next few weeks before the Bolsheviks have time to concentrate their forces, taken from the Eastern and Southern fronts (which they have already started doing) to throw them over Finland and the Scandinavian countries, by which England herself would be threatened. We possess the full particulars of this Bolshevik plan.

Great Russia with Petersburg and Mosco (sic) have so reached the limit of human endurance, under the despotic rule of the Bolsheviks, that they are now ready even to accept help and salvation at the hands of Germany. German agents are already fully at work all over Russia offering with true German precision, point by point, all help for present and future – in fact are preparing themselves an alliance with Russia, which, if the Allies continue in their present unreliable politics towards us, will inevitably be accepted by all anti-bolshevik parties independent of their political views and feelings. Such a result would ultimately enable Germany to throw off and annul the obligations of the treaty of Versailles.

Russia, once liberated from the Bolsheviks and more or less in working order has sufficient food supplies to feed herself and Germany for years to come, thereby rendering any future blockade of Germany ineffective. I have been asked to impress the necessity that all the above mentioned negotiations with General Mannerheim and his Ministry should be kept absolutely secret.

The present moment is of vital importance especially from all points of view of the League of Nations.

Bolshevism puts an end to all true democracy, not to talk of the unrealizable socialistic ideal. In asking for assistance against bolshevism one cannot sufficiently insist on the fact that the Allied Governments are not asked to help retrograde Imperialism but are fighting for the people and for true democracy independent of their future form of Government. It is all important that such countries which still have sound Governments should keep control over the present social evolution so that these Governments themselves should not reach that stage of dissolution which hands over the power to the rabble as happened in Russia.

General Gough at the head of the English Military Mission here is fully acquainted with the Military and political situation in Finland and has inspired all parties here with full confidence.

With many thanks for your last kind letter, please believe me dear George

Your devoted cousin,

(Signed) DUCKY.

LETTERS

Russia – Negotiations for the Exchange of Prisoners of War and Repatriation of Civilians

Letters from Maxim Litvinov, Arthur Henderson and Early Curzon were discovered in a cache of letters and documents in the home of O'Grady's granddaughter, Patricia Ventham, after her death.

This collection has been given to the Imperial War Museum and will form the basis for a research site in the Museum under the name O'Grady. See the letter from the Documents Department at the Museum.

FROM THE DEPARTMENT OF COLLECTIONS

Documents and Sound Section

IMPERIAL WAR
MUSEUM

Mrs Diana Giles
Tanyard Cottage
Brook Street
Cuckfield
West Sussex
RH17 5JJ

Imperial War Museum
Lambeth Road
London SE1 6HZ

Telephone 020 - 7416 5223
Fax 020 - 7416 5374
E-mail arichards@iwm.org.uk

APR/DOC1

31 August 2011

Dear Mrs Giles

Thank you for taking the trouble to visit the Museum earlier today, when you kindly left with me the original copies of the letters and associated paperwork kept by your late grandfather, James O'Grady MP, during his negotiations for the exchange of military prisoners following the First World War. It was a pleasure to meet you and I hope that you found your trip rewarding.

We are always keen to look after original documents of this kind in order to ensure that they are preserved under the archival conditions necessary for future generations to study them. Your grandfather's papers reveal an abundance of important information on the prisoner exchange which researchers will undoubtedly find of significant historical value and I should therefore be pleased to accept the collection as a donation to this Museum's archive, where the documents will now be catalogued under your grandfather's name and made available for study.

We remain most grateful to you for your generosity.

Yours sincerely

A. Richards

Anthony Richards
Head of Documents and Sound

*Written to request
permission to publish
in Life of Sir James O'G
J.P., K.C.
23. 3. 2017*

Foreign Office,

6th March, 1920.

Sir,

I desire to offer you my congratulations on the
conclusion of the agreement which you have negotiated at
Copenhagen with a Representative of the Russian Soviet
Government for the exchange of British and Russian
nationals in the British Empire and Russia.

His Majesty's Government consider that you have
successfully carried out the mission with which they
entrusted you, and you will have earned the gratitude
of a large number of our fellow-countrymen for negotiating their release from imprisonment and detention in
a foreign land. I thank you, on their behalf, for your
services.

I look forward to the agreement being carried out
promptly and unreservedly on both sides, as soon as the
practical arrangements for its execution can be completed.

I am,

Sir,

Your most obedient,

humble Servant,

James O'Grady Esq., M.P.

CHAPTER III

THE AFTERMATH OF REVOLUTION
FAMINE

Fotogrāfs R.Johanson)   Fotografēšanas 19‾?.gadi
                                            laiks

Apraksts Raiņa bulvāris.Priekšplānā Lielbritānijas vēstniecības ēka.
          Melnbalts,stikls 13 x 18 cm

Fig 1 *The British Legation in Riga*

In November 1921, O'Grady was appointed by the International Federation of Trade Unions, head of their Famine Relief Commission. (*See* Appendix VI.)

Regrettably we have not succeeded in obtaining a copy of the report O'Grady will undoubtedly have made to the Federation on completion of his administration of this Fund in Russia. Many of the organisations involved have searched their archives – it may no longer exist.

We have the letter dated April 12th 1922 from Mr. E.G. Wilton of the British Legation in Riga (Fig 1) to Lord Curzon, then British Foreign Secretary, advising that O'Grady had passed through Riga a few days earlier:

"My Lord Marquess,
I have the Honour to report that ....
In addition to the better-known relief Schemes there are also two others which have only recently come to my notice. A few days ago Mr. O'Grady M.P. called to see me on his way to Moscow and informed me that a relief centre had been started last winter in Chuvash, about 50 miles from Kazan, with Trade Union subscriptions amounting to over £50,000. He related to me that his organization was somewhat contemptuously styled "the Yellow International" by the Bolsheviks, but he seemed to be in good relations with them and made no complaint of lack of assistance in forwarding his supplies. There is also a second scheme called "German Third International" which proposed to work among the German colonies along the Volga. I am informed that the director has gone made and the others seem to be existing in a state of feverish muddle. I am told that the German colonists who survive have no desire to be "helped" by this Society and would rather trust to their own poor efforts and the small succour which comes their way from the Government.
According to my information, the amount of sowing in the famine areas is about one-quarter of the normal amount. The autumn sowing prospects are, speaking generally, fairly good; those of the spring sowing less so, not only on account of the shortage of seed but, also, the scarcity of beasts for ploughing and transport. This scarcity varies in different parts from a complete dearth to a fairly respectable average; for example, in the Buzuluk area, where camels are used, transport is moderately good. Generally speaking, little hay is left anywhere in the famine regions and the miserable animals are eking out their existence on dried thistle stalks.
It is difficult to give even an approximate estimate, but my information leads me to believe that, even under favourable conditions, the July and August harvests in the Volga zones will be inadequate to feed more than from 1/3 to 1/2 of the 15 or 20 million inhabitants. The fraction, however, is likely to approximate to 1/2, in consequence of the progressive mortality from hunger and disease; for example, it is probable that during the month of March 2 per cent of the population in the famine area has died. Owing to the difficulties of sending relief, it is also possible that death and migration will reduce the country to the east of Saratoff into a vast desert this year; in normal times, this region was fertile and produced an abundance of wheat. I hear also that the conditions the Ukraine are bad and that the prospects of famine are not remote.
I have the honour to be, ..."

This gives a fairly clear picture of the situation in the Famine Area.[6]

On his return to England, O'Grady passed round in the House of Commons a piece of famine 'bread' which was partly composed of clay.

According to the Dictionary of Labour Biography, O'Grady travelled to Russia again in 1922 (*see also* Part IV Conclusion) returning in time for Christmas with his family.

Cousin Joan recalls (16.11.2002):

December 1922

Grandpa (James O'Grady) came home from Russia just before Christmas. He was not very well but it was thought that, because he had witnessed so many scenes of starvation and disease, he was just 'run down' as a consequence.

He was sitting in his chair by the fire on Christmas Day; all the family was gathered together in 60 Cavendish Road. At that time Joan and Kathleen were the only grandchildren in England; Grandpa, always loving and affectionate, had one child on each knee his arms wrapped around them, talking to them.

The next morning, Boxing Day, he was very unwell; Grandma (Louise) didn't like the look of the rash on his forehead and, mindful of his visit to Russia, she called Dr. Steele, the family Doctor. He came quickly and seeing the condition of James, he telephoned St. Thomas Hospital. Within a few hours James was in hospital and smallpox had been diagnosed.

After that it was All Systems Alert; by evening all the family members and everyone who had been in contact with James were lined up to be vaccinated, including the children who were wakened from their beds.

Everyone was isolated for two or three weeks; the milkman and baker left their deliveries by the gate.

Important papers for Grandpa to sign were collected and fumigated.

The children were allowed to go walking with their mother but not to go into the shops or have any contact with the people in the streets. While out walking one day, Joan recalls seeing the News placard announcing "M.P. with Smallpox".

James made a complete recovery due to the swift action of his wife Louise and his doctor, Dr. Steele.

No one else contracted the disease in the family or amongst friends.

---

6 *See also* Appendix VII – *Soviet Russia, The Road to Famine from The Pageant of the Years* by Philip Gibbs

Among O'Grady's papers we found a wallet which he must have taken with him on his journey to the famine areas. It contains bank notes from many of the countries on his route, including one for 10000 Marks (Reichsmark note). (*See* below).

Examples of currency carried by James O'Grady during his 1921 Russian visit

CONCLUSION

It is reported that O'Grady was involved in the matter of German reparations to Russia and in this regard we have a copy of a communication from the British Legation in Riga to the Foreign Office in London, as follows:

> Riga April 12 1922
> My Lord Marquess,
>   In my confidential despatch No. 103 I had the honour to refer to the visit of Mr. James O'Grady M.P. on April 6th. Mr O'Grady was accompanied by colonel Hon. F. Cripps who is, I believe, a stepson of Lord Parmoor. The latter informed me that he was proceeding to Moscow with Mr. O'Grady and stated that his business there was in connection with a deal in which German interests, especially Krupps, were bound up: Krupps, he added, were anxious to obtain supplies of raw materials from Russia. Colonel Cripps incidentally referred to the survey of the port of Petrograd made by British firms a year or so ago, and seemed to think there was an eventual possibility of arriving at some satisfactory conclusion in this matter.
>   I have the honour to be, etc ......

His visits to Russia in 1922 were probably therefore dual purpose, ie, to carry out his responsibilities with regard to famine relief and to be involved in the deals between Russia and Germany.

In this regard, we do know that, in 1924, Ramsay MacDonald was anxious to resume trade with Russia as a means of reducing unemployment in this country and was, therefore, intending to reopen relations between Russia and Great Britain.

It was announced in the *London Gazette* that O'Grady was to be appointed the first British ambassador to the Soviet Union.

However, in the autumn of 1924, the Zinoviev letter was "leaked". (*See* over, p60.) This led to the downfall of the first Labour government in September. The Conservative government which then took office, did not wish to send an ambassador to the Soviet Union at that stage.

O'Grady was subsequently offered the post of Governor of Tasmania.

This was, of course, a great honour, but it was also exile for J. O'G and seems to have been a great waste of the talents he had acquired and of his knowledge and experience of Russia and the situation which had developed there during the revolution and Civil War and their aftermath.

Finally, I give copy of a letter dated 21st July 1917 from Lord Stamfordham to J. O'G (*see* over, pp58–9) in reply to his letter from which it would appear that J. O'G had an unrealistic view of the future of Bolshevism in Russia.

We know that the Bolsheviks had a very limited following and, had Kerensky been a stronger character and dealt more ruthlessly with the Bolshevik uprising in July 1917, J. O'G's optimism would have been well founded.

And so ended O'Grady's involvement with Russia – perhaps the most important and interesting part of his life's work, lasting over a period of nine years.

BUCKINGHAM PALACE

21st.July 1917.

Dear Mr O'Grady,

It was very good of you to write
to me, and the King has read your letter with
interest.

You were certainly a right prophet about
Brussiloff's Army taking the offensive: and it
has been successful if only it can keep what it
has gained.

I quite understand what you say about the
numbers killed in the streets of Petrograd: they
really are insignificant in a country with Russia's
enormous population, and I think everyone has
realised that more bloodshed was inevitable ere
things could settle down. Indeed we may reasonably
look for further sacrifice of life before the new
Russian Government is secure in the saddle.

.

-2-

It looks as if Lenin thought it was well to make himself **scarce**, and it is quite possible **we** may not hear of him again in Petrograd.

I hope to have the chance of another talk with you before long.

Their Majesties are going to Aldershot to get a little of that good **air**, and **a** comparative rest as they have been doing a great deal lately.

Yours very truly,

Stamfordham

James O'Grady Esq:
       M.P.

The Zinoviev Letter

According to the files of the OGPU's Foreign Department, no special investigation was conducted into the origin of that most mysterious of documents, the Zinoviev letter, which played such a decisive role in the downfall of Britain's first Labour government and led to the Conservative victory in the general election of October 1924. Timely publication in the press of what purported to be an undisguised incitement to revolution and mutiny, supposedly despatched to British Communists by the Comintern leader Grigori Zinoviev on the eve of the polls, helped to destroy Ramsay MacDonald's chances.

The absence of an OGPU mole-hunt implies that there was no leak of a genuine document, and it is clear from the archive that the key to the story lies in the flow of agent reports on the activities of a group of forgers among White Guards officers, based mainly in Berlin. Among them, the principal personality who interested the OGPU was Vladimir Grigorievich Orlov, the former chief of intelligence of General Wrangel's army who, after the end of the Civil War, was engaged in fabricating and selling Soviet and Comintern documents as well as preparing his own intelligence bulletins. The OGPU was particularly well-informed about his activities, as is evident from a note in Orlov's dossier, dated 19 March 1929, which states that 'constant taps were kept on Orlov's activities by our sources A/3 and A/25'.[1] However, these activities represented only the tip of the iceberg; the main part of Orlov's work, running a White Guard network of agents abroad, remained concealed until 1945, when new information made it possible for the Soviets to build an accurate retrospective assessment of what Orlov had been up to twenty years earlier. Just as Berlin was being liberated, the Head of the 9th Department of the NKVD's First Directorate, Gukasov, reported in a note dated 23 April 1945 and addressed to the Chief of Intelligence, Pavel Fitin, that the Paris *rezidentura* had seized in Belgium the archives of the former chief of 'the intelligence unit of the Russian General Staff' and was sending them to Moscow.[2]

From The Crown Jewels by Nigel West and Oleg Tsarev

Ramsay MacDonald, the Labour Prime Minister. After the letter was
published his party lost by a landslide, but attracted a million more votes

12 THURSDAY, FEBRUARY 4, 1999   *

NEW

A famous mystery has been partly solved, writes **Michael Smith**

Zinoviev letter was a fake, inquiry admits

THE so-called Zinoviev Letter was a forgery, a year-long Government investigation has confirmed.

The investigation, prompted by documents released by the former KGB and published last year in *The Daily Telegraph*, concluded that the letter was widely leaked by MI6 and MI5 to discredit the Labour Government.

The letter, leaked days before the 1924 election, was a call from the Soviet leadership to Britain's communists asking them to "mobilise sympathetic contacts" inside the Labour Party. It lost the election by a landslide.

But the KGB files, released to *The Daily Telegraph* in Moscow, show that although the sentiments were genuine, the letter was a forgery.

Dr Gill Bennett, the Foreign Office chief historian, was given access to all the secret British files on the letter, including an MI5 investigation of its provenance and to the KGB archives in Moscow.

Although she accepted the evidence of the KGB files, published by the spywriter Nigel West and former KGB officer, Oleg Tsarev, as *The Crown Jewels*, she declined to confirm that the forgery was commissioned by MI6.

"The idea of an institutionalised international campaign, directed by MI6, to discredit both the Bolsheviks and the Labour Government is not only unsubstantiated by the documents, but seems inherently unlikely," she said. Nevertheless, she conceded that a number of officers from MI6 and MI5 were

Grigory Zinoviev and Gill Bennett. Below, how the 'plot' was announced in the Daily Mail in 1924

involved in leaking the forged letter and that both agencies actively circulated it among Government departments.

"It may have suited certain persons to leak the letter," Dr Bennett said. "It probably was leaked by members of MI6 to Conservative Party Office."

The main person responsible for this is named as Desmond Morton, then in charge of intelligence production within MI6, but later better known as intelligence adviser to Prime Minister Winston Churchill during the Second World War. But Dr Bennett also blames MI5 and in particular Joseph Ball, a senior officer who would

later become Director of Information for Conservative Party Central Office.

"In circulating the letter, MI5 would have been well aware that it could only be a matter of time before it was leaked to the press," she said. "Its incitement to insubordination and revolt in the Armed Forces was bound to have a powerful impact on men who were already impatient at the refusal of successive governments to denounce Soviet propaganda and subversive activities."

The Zinoviev Letter was alleged to have been written to the British Communist Party by Grigori Zinoviev, the head of the Comintern,

the organisation set up by Moscow to control communist activity abroad.

The letter, which called on the British Communists to mobilise "sympathetic forces" in the Labour Party, was leaked to the *Daily Mail* shortly before the October 1924 general election.

The newspaper spread details of the letter across its front page, headlined: "Civil War Plot By Socialists' Masters; Moscow Orders To Our Reds; Great Plot Disclosed".

In fact, it is not clear what effect the letter had on the election. Despite its defeat, the Labour vote rose by a million. It was the mass defection of Liberal votes to the Conservatives that handed them victory.

But the letter has continued to cause controversy with persistent claims that it was a forgery aimed at preventing Ramsay MacDonald, the Labour Prime Minister, from gaining a second term.

The KGB files show that the letter was forged by a White Russian emigre in the Latvian capital Riga at the behest of MI6.

The most likely reason appears to have been to protect a high-level MI6 source within the Soviet leadership who was reporting information remarkably similar to that reproduced in the Zinoviev Letter.

But Dr Bennett concludes that it remains impossible to confirm the true origins of the Zinoviev Letter and that it remains as one newspaper said at the time, "a most extraordinary and mysterious business".

ENTR'ACTE

Early in 1924, O'Grady received the following letter from the Prime Minister, Ramsay MacDonald. This, however, was followed by some rather unhappy correspondence as below. I give also the offending news report.

Copy.

Friday.

Private & Confidential

My dear O'Grady,

I am proposing to offer you Moscow when the Russian Government is recognised, & so shall not suggest any office to you at present. I hope you will approve.

Yours very sincerely,

(signed) J. Ramsay MacDonald.

10, Downing Street,
Whitehall, S.W.

13th March, 1924.

PRIVATE & CONFIDENTIAL.

My dear O'Grady,

     I am very much distressed about this Russian affair altogether, but it was considerably added to by the fact that, on the day after I saw you, the "Evening Standard" had a paragraph which bore on the face of it traces of inspiration. Your very words were reproduced in it. Instead of helping, all this is only hindering.

     I wish further to put it in writing that the objection is not on the ground of diplomacy or anything of that kind. It is simply that I have been informed that they will not have you. I have done my best and am continuing to do so, but things have got to a point when I have had to warn you that I may find it quite impossible to force you upon them.

                Yours very sincerely,

                J. Ramsay MacDonald

J. O'Grady, Esq., M.P.

March 14th, 1924.

Dear Prime Minister,

Your letter of the 13th distresses me very much. I knew nothing re the paragraph in the "Evening Standard" until my attention was drawn to it by Sir Philip Dawson in the Smoke Room. I was angry and immediately attempted to see you on that evening to again point out that someone in the "F.O." - antagonistic to myself - was giving information to the Press.

Quite obviously I would not give information to the Press that was against my interests, and the paragraph in question is of that nature. I would give much to discover, as I am sure you would, the source of the leakage.

15th March, 1924.

Dear Prime Minister,

I have again read the paragraph in
the "Evening Standard"-cutting enclosed-and
I do not find anything in it that led you to
the conclusion that in a way I was responsible.

As far as I remember our conversation
on Monday last, there does not seem to be any
reference to the course that conversation took.

You certainly did not mention Chicherir
as having objected to myself. Indeed I thought
it might be Kamenev. However, that is neither
here nor there. The par. in question does not
in any way favour myself and, were I responsibl
I should be not only a fool but a stupid fool
I again repeat I have had nothing to do with
pressmen-neither has anyone in my Union Office
or at my home. I schooled my people very well
in that matter.

I have sent the paragraph to Ponsonby
asking him to trace it to its source.

Yours sincerely,

I have never for a moment had a

thought in my mind that there was any other

intention than that stated in your first

letter to me on the matter, and am content

to leave it on the understanding suggested

when I saw you in your room in the House of

Commons.

moment has come, and the policy is not there. Mr. Shaw is even angry that a policy should be expected of him.

Assuredly, there is no disposition in any quarter to censure the Government because, in seven weeks of existence, it has not formulated some immense scheme for dealing fundamentally with the unemployment problem in all its difficulties and complexities. The Parliamentary Opposition and the country are perfectly reasonable on that point. But when the Minister of Labour is driven to say that "the only real remedy (for unemployment) is the restoration of foreign trade" it is impossible to avoid a comparison between the very official style of Labour in office and the uncharitable and hypercritical attitude it assumed in Opposition.

While, however, the Government offers no proposals dealing with the fundamentals of the unemployment question, it is using its administrative powers to extend the classes to whom unemployment allowances are paid. Mr. Shaw holds that "every unemployed man and unemployed woman in this country has a "right" to live." The emphasis is on the word "right." Not the sternest individualist, we imagine, would claim that temporary or permanent failure should involve starvation. But the assertion that every individual has a "right" to be maintained by the State in a position not inferior in comfort to that of many actual workers is a quite different matter. It is, of course, possible to conceive that, under a very different polity from any with which the world

Chamberlain just before he went out of office, when he confessed that the Exchequer had paid back more money than it had received. The repeal of the clause will, it is hoped, stop this drain on the Treasury.

Mr. O'Grady Turned Down.

The Russian Government has exercised a well-understood diplomatic right in indicating that it would prefer a professional diplomatist as British Ambassador in the place of Mr. O'Grady.

This right has been exercised in our own country on more than one recent occasion, and also in other parts of Europe. It is unfortunate that the experience of Mr. O'Grady, who has paid several visits to Russia already on Government missions, should not be utilised, but otherwise M. Chicherin's objection seems sound.

Mr. MacDonald's Government cannot last for ever, and if it were to be succeeded by one which took a slightly different view with regard to Russia, a professional diplomatist would probably be more useful in Moscow than an Ambassador, as Mr. O'Grady would be, of the American type who is known to be attached to a particular party.

Baptism in the Crypt.

Mr. Macpherson had clearly right on his side in the short speech which he made on the Government last night about the baptism of his son.

Like the Abbey itself, the chapel in the crypt of the House of Commons is not under Church jurisdiction at all, and Canon Carnegie seems not only unwise, but acting in a position of very doubtful validity in refusing to allow a baptism to take place there according to the rites of the Established Church of Scotland.

I trust that Lord Lincolnshire, who as Lord Great Chamberlain is in charge of the Royal Palace of Westminster, will soothe Mr. Macpherson's feelings and allow the ceremony to take place as he wishes.

It does seem unreasonable that in a chapel

for this country, not only because, as usual at this season, most of those travelling in the sleeping cars appear to have been English and English people have lost their lives, but because it raises doubts which travellers accustomed to our own railway methods must often have felt regarding the high speeds commonly attained on French lines.

Since the war there have been a number of railway accidents in France, partly due, no doubt, to an inevitable deterioration of material, but also in some cases to sabotage.

Dangerous Speed.

There seems no reason to look for the cause of the present accident in either of these directions. The train was simply going too fast at certain points and got derailed in consequence.

Considering the vast volume of traffic carried on the P.L.M., their proportion of accidents has not been great, nothing like so high, for instance, as on the State Ouest line when it was taken over by the Government. I remember well many years ago its celebrating its transference to national hands by nearly killing Mr. Arnold Bennett.

Major Hore-Belisha.

I am sorry to hear that Major Hore-Belisha, who beat Sir Clement Kinloch-Cooke at Devonport during the election, has been seriously ill and is ordered abroad for several weeks.

Major Hore-Belisha, who is one of the most promising of the younger M.P.s, has already one Parliamentary distinction.

He has asked more questions than anybody else—indeed, he has each day had the maximum allowed him on the paper.

M. Caillaux Comes Back.

M. Caillaux is still obliged to live outside Paris and unable to hold any public office as a result of the sentence passed upon him during M. Clemenceau's Premiership in the war.

None the less, it is natural that French public opinion should begin to show tendencies of turning towards the man who, rightly or wrongly, has had the reputation of having the best financial brain in French politics, and

praises of d'Annunzio, Maeterlinck, Puccini, Ostorini, Respighi and their like, Mme. Ileana Leonidoff-Massera does not lay the entrancing Russian ghosts who dance for most of us still at Covent Garden. This, however, is not to say that she is not charming or that she does not dance delightfully. She is and she does.

An eighteenth-century Venetian frolic to Boccherini went best last night. In the more ambitious Persian Feast the movements of the corps de ballet were a little tedious, and the Rimsky Korsakoff Hindu Song is more than a little hackneyed.

A porcelain piece, with Mme. Leonidoff-Massera herself as the Camargo, was charming. As a pas seul, Mme. Leonidoff-Massera dances Ophelia's mad scene to the Sibelius Valse Triste, which "goes," curiously well to the familiar movements of this scene.

The Gondoliers.

There was no probable possible shadow of doubt that "The Gondoliers" enjoyed a regular royal success at the Prince's Theatre last night.

It is one of the gayest of the Gilbert and Sullivan series, contains some of the most familiar and delightful melodies, and is interesting musically because of the exceeding deftness of Sullivan's orchestration.

Its Audience.

And how interesting a study is the audience! I find my fellow-playgoers there markedly different from those I see in any other theatre.

For one thing, barring a few deadheads in the way of critics, they have all paid to go in, an unusual and cheerful circumstance in London stalls.

They approach the operas with an almost grave adoration, but they do not decide the encores. Apart from one little lapse into a really tempestuous enthusiasm which held up the Grand Inquisitor (Mr. Leo Sheffield) for a moment, they obeyed the generous decisions of the conductor in this matter without question.

What is the Right Cigarette Ration?

PERSONAL & PRIVATE.   10, DOWNING STREET,
                                       WHITEHALL, S.W.

                                       17th March, 1924.

My dear O'Grady,

          I have yours of the 15th instant.

          The first paragraph of the cutting was one
of the points we discussed, and it reproduced in its
form a mistake which you made in misunderstanding what
I said to you. What happens in these interviews is
this: that something is said to somebody, who goes and
says it to somebody else, and then it gets in the press.
I wish again to emphasise that there is no question of a
professional diplomatist involved. It certainly does
not come from the Foreign Office, as the Foreign Office
knows nothing about it and has not been interesting
itself in the subject. The only possible explanation
is incautious talk. However, the matter must remain
where it is until the Conference begins here.

                    Yours very sincerely,

                    J Ramsay MacDonald

J. O'Grady, Esq., M.P.

My Dear O'Grady
     Thanks for yours. much
will have to be done yet
before I can think y appointing
an Ambassador to Moscow.

It all seems a storm in a teacup. The Labour government fell from office in September and as the Tories had no wish for diplomatic representation in Moscow, the matter ended there.

Shortly afterwards, O'Grady was offered the post of Governor of Tasmania which he accepted, as also a Knighthood – KCMG. Some of his fellow Labour members thought he should refuse the latter, but he accepted it as a 'great honour'.

On the occasion of his 'dubbing', he told the King (George V) that he felt overwhelmed by the solemnity of the occasion. 'Then,' said the King, 'go and sit down; I'll be with you shortly and we'll talk about cabinet making, your kind, not mine.'

PART V

TASMANIA
by Ian Walden, edited by Diana Giles

Introduction

In the summer and early autumn of 1924, with the MacDonald government reaching its final days, it was already clear that the foreseeable future was likely to see little further progress on Anglo-Soviet diplomatic or trade relations. As such, at 58 years of age, a new outlet was required for O'Grady's international experience and skill. While the government suffered its final crisis, he was being asked to consider accepting an appointment as His Majesty's imperial representative in the state of Tasmania. By 10th October the London *Daily Express* was able to report that the obstacle of finances sufficient to enable a Governor to maintain Government House and exercise his duties, had been successfully overcome. O'Grady consequently confirmed that he would not contest his parliamentary seat in South-East Leeds. Within a week of the General Election that saw Stanley Baldwin's Tories returned to power, he was kneeling before King George V to receive his knighthood and formal appointment as Governor. Less than two months later, on a chilly summer morning shortly before Christmas 1924, Sir James was sailing into Launceston harbour to take up his new role.

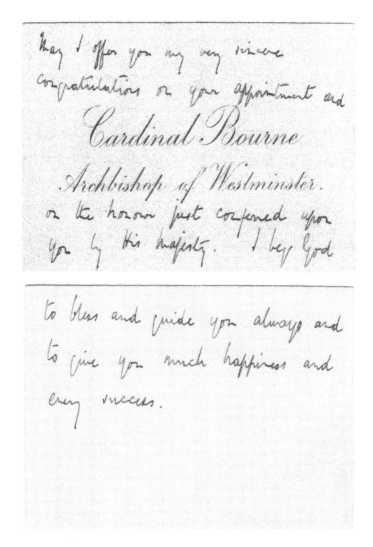

Shortly before sailing (for Tasmania), Sir James received this card from the
Cardinal Archbishop of Westminster

Arrival in Tasmania

Change, particularly rapid change, always brings sacrifices as well as
new hopes. By far the hardest aspect of this new role was Lady O'Grady's
inability, due to ill health, to accompany her husband on the long journey
to their new home. At the time, Louie was able to write "very cheerfully
and hopefully," and there were hopes that, after an operation expected

to be performed in May 1925, she would soon recover sufficiently to be reunited with him. Little did anyone then suspect that hope for Louise's recovery would be abandoned two years later, and that on 24th April 1929, before Sir James could return home, her struggle with illness would come to an end.

In the meantime, the new Governor of Tasmania was accompanied by two of his daughters. Molly brought with her two children, Mary, aged 5, and John, then 3½, as well as invaluable recent experience of life in Tasmania. After the war, upon her husband's demobilization from naval service, they had purchased an orchard near Latrobe, and had lived there for several years, during which time John was born. While Molly's sojourn was to be relatively short, at most two years, Margaret, then aged only 19, would ultimately remain by her father's side, as personal support and *de facto* first lady, throughout his time as Governor.

There would be little private time for the family to settle in. Their ship, the *Nairana*, was greeted by a crowd of many hundreds shortly before 8am on Tuesday 23rd December, 1924. The party did not even have a chance to disembark before various town dignitaries and members of the press corps converged to get a glimpse of their King's representative, to hear what he had to say, and present official messages of welcome. Such enthusiasm was understandable. It had been almost three years since their previous Governor, Sir William Allardyce, had left the State to take up the Governorship of Newfoundland, and Tasmanians had been without a Governor since then. The constitutional aspects of the role had been performed by a local Administrator (the most recent of whom, Sir Herbert Nicholls, had recently been appointed Lieutenant-Governor), but the vital human link with King and Empire had been sorely missed. Sir James was well prepared to meet the expectant crowds, bringing a message from the King of fond remembrance of the last Royal visit, with sincere hopes for the island State's increased prosperity, and a reassurance that their loyalty and sacrifice in war-time had not been forgotten at the centre of Imperial power.

No time was available for relaxation or sight-seeing in this new home. By mid-afternoon that first Tuesday the family, accompanied by Sir James' aide-de-camp Captain Percy Wright, had arrived in Hobart by train. Here also the weather was failing to match the drama of the occasion; it may have been high summer, but the day was blustery, full of chill showers and leaden skies. The vice-regal party would have to wait to see the famed views over the river Derwent in all their glory. A more weather-proof attraction, however, was Government House itself, a beautiful residence, and one into which Sir James was immediately ushered for the swearing-in ceremony. In the relatively shielded and confined surrounds of the study, in the presence of the members of the Cabinet, Sir James presented his commission as Governor to Mr Justice Crisp, who administered the oaths of allegiance and office. The brief ceremony was concluded by Sir James' signing of the official proclamation announcing that he had assumed the administration of the Government.

The following day, a much warmer and sunnier one, Sir James made his official entry into the city of Hobart, decked out in full official regalia. Travelling slowly by car from Government House through the bunting-strewn and crowd-filled streets, he was brought to the town hall. Here the mayor, Alderman F.D. Valentine, the state Premier, Hon. J.A. Lyons, and other officials were present to welcome Sir James to the official public levee. To this event, all citizens were invited to come and pay their respects to their King's representative, and Sir James was personally introduced to a large number of people, both private citizens and those representing branches of city and state government, the church, and the business community. Addresses of congratulations and assurances of loyalty were made on behalf of many of these bodies, in response to which Sir James gave a speech of personal introduction. He thanked them for their messages of welcome, expressed his pride in being part of the Empire to which the world currently looked for leadership, delight at being in Tasmania as an expression of his (typically Irish) thirst for adventure, and his intent to listen, to serve by giving advice, and to explain his actions whenever asked. He acknowledged that he would make mistakes, and warned his audience that he never attempted to excuse his conduct. He concluded by repeating the King's happy memories of his visit to Tasmania, and his keen personal interest in the development of their State.

Events to welcome and honour the new Governor continued to be held in various places for almost a month, including a further public reception in Hobart where some 1,500–2,000 people gathered to greet the whole vice-regal family. On Sir James' first official visit to Launceston, on 23rd January 1925, the City Council thoughtfully presented a gift for Louise, a portfolio of views of Launceston and Northern Tasmania, to help her feel connected to her husband's work and to enable her to anticipate her future home.

Press coverage of Sir James' arrival, particularly in the island's two major newspapers, the Hobart *Mercury* and the Launceston *Examiner*, was characterised by expressions of loyalty towards the King's representative, and personal goodwill toward a man they perceived to be genial, business-like, approachable, straightforward, and eager to be of practical service to the people of Tasmania. They described him as "a man first and a Governor afterwards" and repeated his request to the populace that they "take me for what I am; no more, and certainly not less."

Duties

In the meantime, Sir James rapidly threw himself into the duties of the Governorship. His principal constitutional roles encompassed the official opening of the State parliament in June each year, the consideration of bills passed by parliament, and the granting of Royal Assent. One of the earliest bills to reach him, in mid-January 1925, was a particularly difficult case. The Land and Income Tax Bill carried amendments from the upper chamber, the Legislative Council, and if given Assent in that form would set a precedent allowing them to continue to amend money bills passed in the Assembly. It was a topic sufficiently important and controversial as to lead Sir James to reserve his decision for a month, pending further consideration, and then to give Assent to the unamended bill, rather than granting Assent immediately, as was normal practice.

Beyond the constitutional aspect of the Governor's role lay the social aspect, into which Sir James entered with great commitment and enthusiasm. As the figurehead of government and the representative of royalty, his presence validated and gave significance to a large range of social and community events through the calendar. Annual highlights included state holiday celebrations and commemorations, major sporting events, and the Royal Agricultural Show. A description of these events gives a flavour of the rhythm of social life of Tasmanians and their Governor.

The major sporting events were the racing of boats and horses, principally summer sports and thus the first events which Sir James encountered, the first being the New Norfolk Regatta, the premier rowing event in the State's calendar. Invariably this featured a luncheon and a speech from the Governor. Similarly, he rapidly adopted the New Year's Day sports festival at the North-cast town of Burnie as part of his regular schedule. In late January each year, Sir James travelled north for the Launceston Cup horse-racing festival at Mowbray. In early February, Tasmania and Sir James played host to the Governor-General of Australia, whose visit was timed to coincide with a series of sporting and social festivities, including the Hobart Cup horse-racing festival at Elwick, the Hobart Regatta (for sailing, rowing, and swimming), a garden party at Government House, and the prestigious annual Victoria League Ball. The horse-racing drew typical crowds of 12,000, and as Sir James noted in 1928, was not merely a sporting fixture, but also a great social event, providing a meeting place for residents of all parts of the State, and indeed the mainland. The Regatta, commemorating Abel Tasman's discovery of the island in 1642, was even more popular, with audiences up to 30,000 strong arriving in Hobart to enjoy the racing, the side-shows, and the fashionable carnival atmosphere. In most years ships of the Australian Navy added to the attractions. In 1925 it included the Australian Inter-State yacht races for the first time, and the Forster Cup was won by a Hobart-designed, built and owned yacht named *Tassie*; a proud triumph for the city and for Tasmania as a whole. *Tassie* would go on to win again in 1926 (Perth), in 1927 (Adelaide), and come second to the same team's successor boat, *Tassie Too* in Sydney in 1928. This sequence of boat-building and racing triumphs contributed greatly to Tasmanian self-confidence, and the respect accorded by other States, during Sir James' time in office.

By the second week in March, summer was at an end, and the final large regatta of the season was held each year at Sandy Bay, just south of Hobart. While the winter featured a large variety of local annual events, it was the Royal Agricultural Show at Elwick that, as the name suggests, most clearly demanded a vice-regal presence. This was another major state-wide institution, already 62 years old in 1925, and drawing crowds of around 20,000 spectators, and exhibitors of livestock, farm machinery, and food produce from all districts.

The Governor's annual duties included presiding at events of State, national and imperial significance. Each New Year, Sir James took the opportunity of writing brief letters or articles for the major newspapers, celebrating the past year's achievements and offering encouragement for the one to come.

Next in the calendar came Anzac Day, on 25 April, which was and is the key moment in the year for all Australians commemorating the sacrifice of those fallen in war and the consequent coming to age of Australia as a nation. In Hobart, the day was typically marked by thousands who turned out to watch the spectacular parade of returned soldiers, the laying of wreaths at the memorial cenotaph, and a service, lightened by the institution of a children's picnic and sports meeting in the afternoon. Each year, Sir James's keynote speech reminded those present of the inspirational bravery shown by those who volunteered to fight, and pledged continuing remembrance and gratitude on behalf of all those, in Britain and around the world, who remained free on account of that sacrifice. He made clear his belief that the best way to honour Tasmania's 522 war dead was to care for their dependents, and to pursue the goal of international peace, rather than harbouring bitterness or enmity, for which they had died. His speeches urged that children should be taught, not shielded from, the horror of war, that they might fear and work to avoid it, and endorsed support and strengthening for the still-feeble League of Nations. In continuity with the Anzac commemorations, the Governor also attended a variety of engagements related to the military, unveiling the new Hobart War Memorial in December 1925, inspecting training camps, and viewing several military gymkhanas and exercises.

Sir James' other major holiday speech was given each year on 24th May, for Empire Day. Begun in 1904 through the guidance of Earl Meath, this day remembered the sacrifice of war, but was characterised predominantly by celebration and gratitude for the freedoms enjoyed under the Imperial flag, and the Governor's speeches were duly patriotic and joyful in tone, stressing the importance of the King as a focal point for unity amidst the diversity of peoples in the Empire, and urging all to use their freedom responsibly, working hard for the good of all and doing their bit to pursue peace and progress for all the world. In addition, Sir James reminded Tasmanians of their unity under the British crown on various other occasions, writing a public birthday message to King George V in June 1925, attending a memorial service for the Queen Mother in December of that year, and six months later unveiling a portrait of her in the Queen Alexandra Hospital, Hobart.

Beyond the regular annual events, the Governor of Tasmania was also required to act as host to many international visitors and representatives from a variety of fields. In April 1925, Sir James hosted a reception at Government House for representatives of Dorman, Long & Co., contractors for the Sydney Harbour Bridge, then under construction, who were visiting the state to inspect the works of their cement supplier at Railton, on the island's north coast.

In August, Hobart was visited by a cruiser squadron on the United States Navy under Rear-Admiral Magruder, to whom Sir James offered official messages of welcome and whose officers he hosted at dinner in Government House. In a newspaper message to the citizenry, he encouraged fraternisation ("democrat meeting with democrat in friendly intercourse") with the officers and crew during their stay. In 1926, it was the Japanese navy, then close imperial allies, who visited Hobart, in the form of a cruiser under Captain Yedahara, and who were guests of honour at the Hobart Regatta that year. A further Japanese visit, a training squadron under Admiral Kobayashi, would be feted in July 1928.

Less militant, but no less serious guests, were the England cricket teams touring Australia in 1924/5 and 1929/30. The former had recently taken a beating in the Ashes tests, but received welcoming hospitality and were effusive in their praise of the TCA ground in Hobart. By contrast, the latter team under Percy Chapman featured some of the all-time greats of the game, including Hobbs, Hammond, Sutcliffe, Jardine, and Larwood, and were feted as exotic and triumphant celebrities. In the autumn of both 1926 and 1930, Australian XIs played Tasmania in Hobart, and were equally impressed by the welcome afforded them.

In March 1927, Dame Nellie Melba visited Tasmania and gave a farewell concert, and was welcomed to Government House by the vice-regal party. In May 1928 a still more spectacular arrival was that of Squadron-Leader Bert Hickler, the famous Queensland aviator who had successfully completed a solo flight from England to Australia in just 16 days. Sir James, along with 10,000 spectators, greeted the airman in Launceston, and again in Hobart, as one who had given Australians pride in their country, and who richly deserved the dinner given in his honour at Government House. December saw Sir James host an extremely aristocratic delegation from the St John Ambulance, who arrived in Tasmania as part of an Australasian tour, publicising the organisation's work via films and talks.

Political visitors during Sir James' tenure included a group of MPs from the parliament of Victoria, whose visit coincided with that of the Australian cricketers, and who were welcomed with a dinner and personalised tour of Government House from Sir James and Margaret. In October 1926, a much larger delegation, numbering around 30 elected representatives from various imperial territories, under the banner of the Empire Parliamentary Association visited Tasmania as part of their fact-finding and best-practice-sharing tour of Australia. While their sojourn in the State lasted only six days, the Governor was heavily occupied in preparations and showing their entourage around, as all record of other public appearances vanishes for around three weeks at this time.

Sir James was soon to discover that the post of Governor also brought with it various *ex officio* charity roles. As Tasmania's living link with the heart of Empire, it was natural that he should be Patron of the Victoria League, which aimed to bind imperial citizens together in bonds of friendship. A patriotic body, it organised the major Empire Day celebrations, welcomed new immigrants to Tasmania from Britain, had schemes to education children in Britain about Tasmania, and vice versa, and was parent organisation for the Boy Scouts and Girl Guides movements. Unsurprisingly, therefore, the Governor also served as Chief Scout, and hosted the Inter-State Boy Scouts of Australia corroboree celebrations in January 1927. In addition, throughout his tenure, he called for special public meetings and dedicated Sundays where ministers and others could advertise the service ethic and useful training boys received as scouts, in a bid to overcome the suspicion of jingoism and militarism evidently still attached to the movement by some parents. Consistent with this attitude of proud but peaceful imperialism, Sir James was an avid supporter of the League of Nations Union, and spoke out in support of the League and of the necessity of winning over Russia and the USA to membership. He challenged the cynics who criticised the League's impotence, urging that it was the only organisation able to create a new kind of diplomacy, focused on issue resolution and avoidance of another war, rather than belligerence and national pride.

While currently at peace, Tasmania was still feeling the effects of the Great War. As President of the Tasmanian branch of the Red Cross Society, Sir James passionately publicised the society's work and appealed for funds. Of particular importance was the Society's offering of care and comfort to those injured and traumatised by war. Most of this work was performed at their 'Repatriation Hospital', where returned soldiers continued to receive physical and mental rehabilitation, and practical aid for living independent and productive lives.

Being elected President of the Tasmanian Royal Society enabled a more cheerful topic of discourse. Here the Governor had the opportunity of speaking out on the importance of scientific study, the pleasure to be derived from studying the natural world or attending public lectures on that subject, and the necessity of Tasmanians broadening their horizons of understanding. In particular, he suggested the Society work closely with government departments, especially agriculture, to foster and promote innovation in farming, and education, where simplified forms of the Society's reports could be made available in state schools, helping children know Tasmania better; a move which may induce them to stay, explore, and enrich it as they grew up.

Exploration
Beyond the expected duties of his post, Sir James, according to the Hull *Daily Mail* of 16 March 1927, traversed the whole Island to attend almost any function anywhere to which he was invited, visiting more places,

events, and communities around the state than any Governor before him. To begin with, there was the busy round of social events, principally in and around Hobart, to which the Governor was routinely invited. The newspapers of the time often recorded the vice-regal itinerary for the forthcoming week, and are full of concerts, especially from visiting or youth bands, dances or balls, typically organised as charity fundraisers, the opening of new schools, and public social events such as the first screening of Cecil B. de Mille's film *The Ten Commandments*.

Ever curious and eager to understand the character and potential of the state he had been appointed to serve, Sir James' visits took him into all aspects of community life. The greatest number of appointments was to the numerous agricultural fairs and livestock shows around the State, of which Sir James visited at least ten every year. This is unsurprising when we remember the high proportion of Tasmanians working on the land in the 1920s, and the difficulties of transport, making such fairs extremely important social gatherings where large numbers of people could be met, listened to, and addressed. Speaking at the National Agricultural and Pastoral Society Show in Launceston, in October 1928, Sir James himself noted that the show was important for several reasons. It brought farmers together to discuss mutual problems and find solutions together. It gave a competitive incentive for improving one's produce. But it also educated townspeople as to what their rural citizens were facing, doing, and achieving, and showed the children of the State what their homeland could produce, and what they might, with work, achieve in future.

Second in prominence were visits and addresses to educational establishments. The occasions for these ranged from opening the smallest country school, through speech nights and prize-giving at technical schools and elite private institutions like Hutchins' Boys', St Virgil's, and St Patrick's Colleges, up to the annual commencement speeches at the University of Tasmania itself. Sir James, who had been compelled through family poverty to leave school and begin work at an early age, was well-placed to highlight to students of all ages what a great opportunity was presented to them in their lessons.

With his long experience in industry and industrial relations, and his understanding of economics, it will come as no surprise that meeting and addressing the business community was of particular interest to Sir James. His first major speech introducing himself and his life's work, in January 1925 was addressed to the Hobart Chamber of Commerce, while three years later, he hosted the annual conference of the Associated Chambers of Australia, praising the businessman's habit of negotiation and compromise, and pressing the Chambers to advise the Government on the impact of policies on trade and other international relations. Sir James was also a regular attender at Rotary Club and Fifty Thousand League functions, urging members to be bold and confident in exploring ways to discover Tasmania's wealth, and to focus their charitable activities and influence for the benefit of voluntary organisations he represented, such as the Scouts. By far his most long-standing affiliation was with the Launceston Commercial Travellers' Association, and his addresses at their annual 'Association Day' celebration each August are a helpful barometer of the growing confidence, and occasional struggles, of the business community.

On receiving his appointment as Governor, Sir James began a programme of research on the assets and potential of the island state. From the first, he was interested in means of extending the economy beyond farming, to produce export goods such as minerals, and provide valuable, harvest-proof employment for Tasmania's young people. To this end, he was an avid visitor of industrial locations around the state, including the valuable power-producing hydro-electric works at Waddamana and Lake Margaret, and the mines at Waratah and Derby for tin extraction, and at Mount Lyell in the West for copper, silver, and gold. He also inspected the large cement works at Railton on the North coast and at Darlington on Maria Island, the Electrolytic Zinc Company's works at Risden at the carbide works at Electrona, as well as a variety of consumer-goods factorise such as those producing chocolate (for Cadbury-Fry-Parnell), cider, furs, and tyres. The latter two examples were new start-up ventures, and attracted commendation from Sir James as to the value of new industry to the state as a whole.

Many of these visits, particularly those to locations far from Hobart, were included within tours deliberately planned to enable Sir James to obtain an overview of the whole State. His party was usually small, including only his daughters, his personal secretary Capt. Wright, and his government-supplied ADC, Capt. Stopp. Such interest from the Governor in provincial affairs was unprecedented, and these tours were typically full of scheduled welcome events at every township visited, to the point of crowding out opportunities for viewing the country itself.

Sir James began quickly, with a brief tour of the North-West coast in February 1925, visiting Latrobe, Railton, and Quamby. The following month he was able to return to the area for a longer visit, journeying through the coastal and agricultural regions of Ulverstone, Burnie, Somerset, Elliott, Wynyard, Waratah, and Yolla, before returning to Launceston. While predominantly occupied with civic welcome events and addresses at schools, Sir James was also able to visit a butter factory at Yolla and the huge tin mine at Mt. Bischoff, near Waratah, as well as major autumn agricultural shows at Ulverstone and Wynyard. Within a few days he was off again, to the East coast, visiting the fruit-growing country of Spring Bay, and the National Portland Cement works at Darlington on Maria Island.

February 1926 saw a major tour that covered both the North-East (visiting the schools, dairies and sports festivals of Scottsdale, Ringarooma, Derby, Fingal, and St Helens), and the 'lost province' of the far West. After a minor car accident on the return journey to Launceston, the Western portion of this tour was made against doctors' orders, and was to prove particularly strenuous. It involved travelling to Burnie, before heading South by train for a full day through Guildford, Zeehan, and the port of Strahan. At every town en route, large crowds gathered to welcome the Governor. Queenstown was to act as a base for a 4-day tour of the area, including numerous school addresses, a guided exploration of the famous and productive Mt. Lyell mines, and a day-trip by steam launch from Strahan, across the vast open space of Macquarie Harbour, and up the Gordon River with its dramatic raw beauty, as far as the spectacular Sir John waterfall. From this tour he took an appreciation of the tourism, timber, and mineral potential of the region, and the great importance of completing a proper road Eastward through the mountains to connect this remote area with Hobart. Sir James was able to return to the area for a more leisurely visit in February 1929, and in June of that year the government duly invited tenders for the completion of the remaining 231 miles of the vital road to Hobart. Such a road was eventually completed in the 1930s, but not properly surfaced for some time after that.

1928 was a quiet year, with visits paid to King Island, a centre for pastoral agriculture in the Bass Straight, in April, and to the far North-Western outposts of Stanley and Smithton, in June of that year. The other major island group in the Bass Straight, the Furneaux Group, received a vice-regal visit in June 1929. Sir James spent the majority of his four days on Flinders Island, travelling with members of the Government's "Fauna Board," who were reviewing the islanders' request for an open game-shooting season. It seems kangaroos were attacking crops in large numbers. Alongside noting the islands' potential for flax, dairy, and poultry production, Sir James made a visit, on Sunday 16th, to the "half-caste reservation" on Cape Barren Island. It appears that despite 6,000 acres of excellent soil, and a temperate climate ideal for agriculture, conditions on the island were squalid. One newspaper reporter accompanying the Governor noted that among the 250–300 residents "the trail of incapacity and shiftlessness is over everything. The number of sub-normal children constitutes a serious problem. Disease is rampant. Poverty, dirt and thriftlessness are the outstanding characteristics of the settlement." The Governor addressed a group of around 50 islanders, urging them to develop their land, to take an interest in their children's health, well-being, education, and discipline. Upon his return, he recommended that specific instruction be given to the more "progressive" families in the community, so that they might enjoy the benefits of such work, and serve as an object lesson to others. Later history indicates that whatever measures were taken were insufficient, and by the 1950s the Government resorted to removing children from their parents that they might attend state schools, one of the most controversial episodes in Tasmanian history.

Sir James' tours of Tasmania were, he said, "practically completed" upon his January 1930 visit, albeit an unofficial one, to Port Arthur, site of one of Australia's earliest penal colonies. Newspapers report his far-sighted suggestions as to the necessity of investing in roads and infrastructure to attract heritage tourism business.

Interruptions

As this account suggests, life as Governor of Tasmania featured a large element of annual routine, regularly repeated events, and entering into the established seasonal life of the island state. There were exceptions, however. In July 1925, Sir James and Margaret were able to make a three-week tour of mainland Australia, visiting Melbourne, Sydney, and Brisbane, and noting the characters of these various cities.

On 31st October of the same year, the pair were able to make a social visit to the home of Lord Stonehaven, the new Governor-General of Australia, and his wife, at their home in Melbourne. The trip lasted four days and was filled with race meetings, balls, and receptions.

Winter of 1926 saw another three-week visit to the mainland, enjoying the hospitality of the governors of Victoria and South Australia, taking a trip up the Murray River, and visiting the cities of Adelaide and Melbourne. In late 1928 and again in November 1929, Sir James would return to the Stonehavens' official residence at Federal Government House for a full meeting of all the State Governors.

However, by far the most august event during Sir James' time in office was the visit to Tasmania, in April 1927, of their royal highnesses the Duke and Duchess of York, the future King George VI and Queen Elizabeth. While lasting only four days in total, the visit was long in the planning and anticipation, and the royal couple's time was filled to the brim with events and opportunities for the crowds to see them. Arriving into Hobart on Saturday 16th April aboard HMS *Renown*, their Royal Highnesses were taken by car to the Town Hall, with the car being rushed in an unseemly manner by the eager crowds during its journey. The whole of Hobart was decked out in its brightest and most welcoming attire, with themed decorated arches spanning the roads and depicting the major products of the state, such as apples, electrical power, wool, and minerals. Following a reception at Government House, the itinerary included Easter Sunday service on the 17th, followed by a visit to the Red Cross Repatriation Hospital, and a train journey to Ross. Here, a private couple were to offer temporary sanctuary to the royals at their country mansion, including a chance to go horse-riding on the Monday morning. The afternoon saw the schedule resumed, with similar civic welcomes in Campbell-Town and Launceston, before the party departed for Melbourne on Tuesday 19th. In its reflections on the visit, the *Illustrated Tasmanian Mail* criticised the packed and monotonous schedule imposed on the visitors, and the unthinkingly emotional patriotism exhibited by the crowds, whom it assumed to be ignorant of "the real benefits of monarchy over presidential executives." However, Sir James was particularly noted for being able to introduce numerous citizens to the royal couple by name "with most surprising accuracy" and the paper concluded that certainly "Tasmania has never had a more popular governor."

Following their tour of the State, Sir James accompanied them to Canberra for the official opening ceremony of the Australian Federal Parliament in its new buildings. In an interview of the time he described the calm and picturesque surroundings of the new Federal capital, and a hope that in such surroundings the claims and needs of each State would be more clearly seen and judicially considered than among the "somewhat confused interests existing at present."

The other major event in the life of the state, a much sadder one, was the disastrous floods affecting large swathes of the island in April 1929. On Thursday 4th, Sir James was in St Mary's, on the East coast, to open the annual show. Heavy rains, and news of more to come, led to his evacuation on the last train to make it out of town. Meanwhile, those same rains had caused the Briseis Tin Mining Company's "Cascade Dam" to burst, causing a wall of water 100ft high to wipe out the north-eastern mining township of Derby, leaving the mine flooded and 14 people dead. By Friday 5th, the continuing rain and the surge of water caused the North and South Esk rivers to flood their banks, submerging suburbs and wharves in the northern capital of Launceston. The large and new Rapson Tyre factory was flooded, and 3,500 people were left homeless. Across the northern half of the state, storms caused towns to lose power, roads and rail bridges to be swept away, and coastal towns like St Mary's, Scamander, Burnie, and many others were cut off from the rest of the island. The rail station at Avoca and the Scamander bridge were both turned to matchwood, and a further eight people died when a motor-truck fell into the river Gawler. When the rail line from Hobart had been patched up, on Tuesday 9th, Sir James travelled to Launceston to survey the damage and to inspect the work of the relief depots there. He received, and conveyed to his people, the many messages of sympathy pouring in from across Australia and beyond, including those from Lord Somers, the Governor of Victoria, Lord Stonehaven, and the King. Huge relief appeals were launched both within Tasmania and across mainland Australia, and were generously supported with funds to help the re-building work.

Sir James' time as Governor was also interrupted by occasional health troubles. Some were short-term and able to be reflected on with a degree of humour. Of particular note are the 'slight abrasions and shock' he suffered when the car in which he was being driven "swerved suddenly to one side of the road and struck a tree" en route from Fingal to Launceston in February 1926. A month later, at the St. Mary's Show, he was able to refer to this incident as "that controversy between him and the trees," which he hoped "had been adjourned … never to occur again."[x] In May of that year Sir James was in hospital for a slight operation to his right hand, to repair the restricted muscular action of the right forearm, which had troubled him for some time. While still recuperating in June, he was nonetheless eager to resume visits and public duties.

More serious illness, in the form of two stomach haemorrhages, enforced a stricter pause to Sir James' public engagements. The first took hold on his return from Melbourne in mid-November 1928, and forced him to rest from public functions until Christmas. The second occurred in April 1930, and enforced a further three-week recuperation period. Between these two occasions came the sad news of Lady O'Grady's death in April 1929, following which Sir James took a further month away from the public eye.

The State of Tasmania

Sir James' unprecedented travels during his six years in office put him in a position to draw unique inferences as to the nature of Tasmania and its people. His public speeches illustrate the state of things he discovered in his tours, and his assessment of them. By July 1926, they were able to take a more positive and congratulatory turn regarding the state's affairs. He had noticed a tendency for more young people to remain on their parents' farms, and for farmers to have confidence to invest in new processes and methods. In March 1927 he told the Oatlands Fair-goers that the mining industry was also looking up, and Tasmania's mineral resources were once again gaining notice in the mainland and in Europe. By November of that year he observed a great improvement of show-grounds, entries, and quality of stock at the Scottsdale agricultural show. April 1928 saw the largest apple shipment ever to leave Tasmania for the UK, setting an Australian record in the process. All of these improvements of fortune and finance meant that by June 1928, the newspapers were able to report that the drift of young people to the mainland had finally been stemmed.

The Governor's Service

Sir James' task as Governor was not an easy one. A lifelong political man and seasoned negotiator, he was now prohibited from making political statements or affecting the parliamentary or democratic processes. In 1928 he was able to look back and jokingly remark that when he was appointed in 1924 "he wondered what the devil he was going to do … Even now he found himself straining to be neutral in political matters, and had a hard task to prevent himself sliding down the slippery slope." As such, Sir James needed to decide early what his approach to the position of Governor would be. He saw his role as one of encouraging the endeavour and publicising the potential of Tasmanians, of connecting them to their imperial brethren around the world, and of urging them to take their place within that world-wide family.

Perceiving the state's great potential, contrasted with the inferiority complex and pessimistic attitude shared by many of its people, Sir James set about stirring them up to appreciate their island's resources, and to take a more confident, assertive and business-like approach to securing their future. He was an unapologetic optimist, repeatedly asserting that "I see no use in being otherwise" and that his was an optimism "founded on facts." After all, as he was fond of pointing out, Tasmania had as much land and a better climate than Scotland, and that country supported a population of 4½ million. He urged them to be angry rather than whimpering, assertive of their rights and ambitious in their goals, adopting a number of slogans that give a flavour of his message to the populace. Examples include "Believe in yourselves, and others will believe in you," and "The world will take you at your own valuation, so place a high value upon yourselves." The attitude he wished to see was succinctly expressed to the Municipal Conference in May 1927, in the words "We do not want any favours from anybody; we have certain assets in this island State; consider them as business propositions and in no other way." His reputation as Tasmania's 'honorary publicity man' even led the Melbourne Argus of 18th September 1926 to publish a tongue-in-cheek, if slightly jealous, poem about him, which read:

As knights of old rode forth to "boost"
Each one his lady fair,
Upholding stoutly in the joust
His Guinevere or Clare;
So to maintain Tasmania's fame,
As if she were a lady,
There comes a knight of honoured name
In bold Sir James O'Grady.

He rides no steed that champs its bit
And paws the ground with rage;
His lance a pen, he scores his hit
Upon the printed page.
The news-sheet is the tilting-ground
Where bold Sir Jimmy throws him
His gauntlet down and glares around
To see who dare oppose him.

"Tasmania fair" (this challenge runs),
"I hold your beauty first;
Who contradict are sons of guns,
Give me the lie who durst!
Your hills are tall, your streams are clear -
In short, you take the biscuit.
Refuses one to say 'Hear, hear,'
I'll run him through the brisket!"

With threat'ning pen in air poised high,
He stands a figure grim.
As all men hasten to reply,
"Your views are dinkum, Jim.
Killarney's lakes no more have worth;
And as for Eden's garden,
Who praised it once should bite the earth
And beg Tasmania's pardon."

So on and on goes bold Sir James
In rhapsodies of praise,
Establishing Tasmania's claims
To loveliness's bays.
He hymns each feature of that isle-
Its woods, its balmy breezes
Seems that even man's not vile
Though every prospect pleases.

And so. Victorian patriots,
Who ever are athirst
To glorify our beauty spots
And "See Victoria First,"
Next time you'd "boost" her wattle-gold,
Her fem-clad gullies shady,
Employ the talents of the bold
And fluent Jim O'Grady.

In his many addresses to the farming community, Sir James recognised the value of food and land as state assets, and farmers as a vital part of the economy, adopting the slogan "Save the farmer and you will save the State." He sympathised with their troubles, acknowledging that given the farmer's uncertain returns, they were due special consideration by Parliament in times of poor harvest, and that they should work with consumers to investigate and eliminate the large revenue share taken by middlemen. However, he refused to condone grumbling or over-reliance on protectionism, encouraging farmers to find their own solutions to life's difficulties, through innovation and collective action. He repeatedly emphasised his belief in the great potential of Tasmania, especially its natural advantages that made it cheaper to produce high-quality produce, of certain kinds, than anywhere else, and that there was nothing to be feared from open competition on world markets. Success required only that Tasmanian people would make the best of those advantages. Specialisation in less weather-dependent products such as fat lambs and dairying, would be important, as would more attention to breeding to produce purified pedigree herds (and the eradication of 'scrub bulls'). Farmers, he said, should pay attention to untried yet potentially more profitable activities such as pig production, investigate if they could start loan programs for expensive machinery, or implement scientific methods to improve yields, especially through cooperation with the Department of Agriculture. Sir James had a vision of Tasmania as "the Denmark of Australia," known for application of research, high quality and thereby sustained demand, particularly for pork and dairy products.

Alongside this focus on high-quality exports, he urged effective and confident advertising of Tasmanian wares, and demonstrating confidence in that quality (or "local patriotism") by themselves buying Tasmanian-made goods wherever possible. If the quality and price were right, he asserted, markets would open up of their own accord. In particular, he strongly urged that the State's resources and assets be published in book form, and circulated to the chambers of commerce and financiers throughout the United Kingdom, where capital sought productive outlets and whence investment in Tasmania would surely follow. The creation of secondary industry would enable the export of higher profit-margin products (such as woollen garments, rather than simply raw wool) and keep capital on the island, providing jobs for young adults and more secure markets and incomes for farmers, too.

Perceptively, Sir James also foresaw the growth of tourism as an industry, and urged greater, more active, and more co-ordinated publicity to attract both tourists and long-term immigrants to Tasmania. He actively supported the car clubs and yachting community who were well-placed to advertise the State's scenic attractions, and urged more Tasmanians to spend their own holidays amid the rivers, lakes and mountains of their own state, particularly on the West coast, rather than leaving for the mainland.

Sir James was an active Governor, not content merely to give advice, and he aimed to provide practical assistance to Tasmanians, within the bounds permitted by his role. He provided active support to business, writing letters to the Yorkshire press, to entrepreneurs and to financiers in England, advertising the quality and cost of materials, and the manufacturing outsourcing possibilities, available in Tasmania. Beginning in July 1926, the Hobart *Mercury* printed a series of articles on Tasmania's future prospects, which Sir James faithfully forwarded to contacts in Britain. On several occasions he promised to be a propagandist in the interests of Australia in general, and Tasmania in particular, after his term of office was completed and he was based in the United Kingdom.

Two practical publicity campaigns in which he took an active role ran under the slogans "Made in Tasmania" and "Back to Tasmania." The former fitted well with Sir James' belief in 'local patriotism,' undertaking as it did to exhibit annually the variety and quality of industrial products made within the State, and to urge people to help their own and their neighbours' employment prospects by buying locally wherever possible, and within the Commonwealth when not. In addition to these regular shows, Hobart was also able to host an Empire Shopping Week in May 1929, and an International Motor Show in July 1930, featuring the land-speed-record-breaking "Golden Arrow;" an event at which the Governor presided and endorsed the purchase of tough Australian-made vehicles. The latter campaign was re-named at Sir James' own suggestion as "Come to Tasmania," conveying confidence that Tasmania's charms and prospects could appeal not only to economic emigrants thinking of return home, but also to new immigrants, mainland tourists, and businesses. As Patron of the movement, Sir James gave a radio address in June 1926 characterising Tasmania as "the natural playground of the Commonwealth," lauding its scenic charms, outdoor sporting attractions, the "romance" of exploring still-virgin wilderness, and the warm welcome of its people. He boasted of these same attractions on his tours of the mainland, and was a willing interviewee for British and Australian publications asking about the State.'

The role of Governor as link to the wider imperial family was one Sir James took extremely seriously. At every opportunity he undertook to praise the liberty and essentially peaceful nature of the British Empire, and instil in Tasmanians, particularly children, a sense of pride at belonging to it, a sense of duty to uphold and preserve its values, and a sense of privilege at being able to access the opportunities its freedoms presented. The values of Empire he returned to with great frequency were those of activity, fair play, justice, freedom of thought, toleration of religious difference, the desire for security without subjugating other nations, and the uniting of many diverse cultures in personal loyalty to the monarch. Frequently, of course, he paid tribute to and expressed the nation's gratitude for the sacrifices of those who had fought during the Great War, noting often that Tasmania had, *per capita*, sent more volunteers to the front, and been awarded more Victoria Crosses, than any other part of the Empire. In such addresses he was careful to remind his fellow citizens of their on-going duty, as beneficiaries of peace and freedom, to care and provide for those injured or bereaved during that conflict.

Their other duty, he reminded them, was to build up and preserve a secure, prosperous, British Tasmania, as a defensive bulwark against possible future aggression from the East. Already in 1925 there was fear stemming from a compact between China, Russian and Japan, and in particular from the latter's growing economic power and hurt dignity, following Western allies' refusal to recognise her people's racial equality. In this context the State's strategic importance needed recognising, since an under-populated Tasmania, with its excellent harbours, would be a vulnerable and attractive launch-point for foreign invasion of mainland

Australia. While being mindful of the need for military defence, Sir James insisted on the need for arms reduction and international co-operation if Australia's, and the world's, future prosperity was to be assured.

In urging Tasmanians to build a society worthy of those who had laid down their lives, he commended a spirit of public and practical service, which he characterised in an address to the Girl Guides as "the gospel of unselfishness." This gospel was indeed underpinned by the Christian faith, which he could testify from personal experience gave individual solace and the perspective of justice and of peaceable dealing to one's community work. It was a spirit that could also be inculcated, and was given power, through education and school sports. Sir James' many speeches to school-children emphasised the opportunities open to them, particularly in the formal education which poverty had denied to him, to expand their horizons and possible usefulness to the community. He urged them to take advantage of Tasmania's excellent facilities through hard work, obedience to their teachers, and loyalty to their school and fellow students, both during and after their school days. Addressing teachers and parents, he also noted the importance of investment in education, particularly from age 16 onwards, in developing character and personality, and enabling future citizens to work and vote intelligently for the good of society, in contrast to the mass suffrage given to uneducated Russians in 1917.

The Governor's role excluded any participation in party politics, a fact on which Sir James remarked on his first arrival in Tasmania, and which regulated his public statements on matters of policy thenceforth. For the vast majority of his time in office, he was able to pursue the aforementioned aims with little interaction with the deliberations and policies of the State parliament.

The only exception came in December 1926, when the lower chamber, the House of Assembly, passed a bill granting tax relief to educational establishments, which was turned down by the upper chamber, the Legislative Council. Sir James, commenting on this exchange at the Hutchins School speech night, was reported by the *Mercury* to have said that he "felt inclined to thank the Government and to say something very strong about the Legislative Council" and that he predicted a "fight" in which the school's headmaster would probably be engaged on the subject. These remarks were seen as a judgement on parliamentary decisions, and as such a 'breach of privilege', not in keeping with the customary role of the Governor or the example of the King, and criticised in Council as "unwise, indiscreet, and improper." Sir James was quick to explain that the newspaper report did not clearly represent his real attitude, which explanation was accepted by the Council, and the affair was over within a few days of its beginning.

Of much longer duration, however, was the continual constitutional debate over the Governorship itself. One aspect of this debate was financial; the State's already over-stretched budget did not permit a generous salary to the Governor. Indeed, an article by the London *Daily Telegraph* of March 24, 1926 described his £2,500 as "meagre" for the upkeep of his establishment. As a result, some of Sir James' expenses, including fuel and light in Government House, an official car to transport him to functions, and Captain Stopp's services as ADC, were soon being covered by special appropriation from other areas of the State funds. This situation lead Premier Lyons to state the Government's aim, in August 1925, that the position of Governor be reduced to an administrative one, focusing on constitutional duties, and thereby saving the expense of many social engagements and travels.

The other issue under discussion throughout Australia in this period was the future restriction of State Governorships to Australian-born citizens. Locals might be exposed to charges of partisan feeling, and might be less effective 'liaison officers' with the United Kingdom. Furthermore, the majority of Tasmanian MPs asserted in October 1925 that no mandate had been received from the people to seek a change on this issue, and voiced their opposition to such a change. However, in spite of such opposition, it seems all the State Premiers apart from Victoria signed a proposal for restriction to the Imperial Government in London. The reply they received from the Secretary for Dominion Affairs refused the change, firstly on the grounds that the existing system allowed maximum freedom to choose Governors born either within or outside Australia. This was to be proved in December 1930, with the appointment of Sir Isaac Isaacs as Governor-General. The second reason, as noted by the *Telegraph* article referred to above, was that the request, coming as it did exclusively from Labour-party leaders, may reflect only "a passing current of opinion among certain sections of trade unionists" and not the general will of the Australian people. While there may have been sympathy in London for a Canadian-style system, whereby the Governor-General appointed State Governors, such a move was strongly opposed by the Tasmanian press, who noted their State's longer connection with London than with the Australian Commonwealth, and a desire to be free of mainland influence in this regard.

Popular reception

When Sir James arrived in Tasmania, he faced something of an uphill struggle. Not only were finances tight and some sentiment abroad opposing appointment of Governors from outside the State, but there were also those who were uncertain what to make of Sir James' well-known background in the labour movement. However, as Sir James was quick to point out, his position was an imperial one, and his political party had a "very glorious" record with regard to matters imperial."

From such beginnings, Sir James went on to prove himself an extraordinarily popular Governor. His relatively humble background, his long service of the working people, his military record, and his distaste for class divisions all helped to endear him to the independent-minded, hard-working, long-sacrificing people in this outpost of Empire. Even the doubters were soon referring to his 'healthy' and 'constructive' brand of socialism. While he himself credited his popularity to Tasmanians' own generous feeling and loyalty to the King he represented, it is clear that as time passed they observed with approval his desire to serve, his enthusiastic participation in the ordinary sporting and social life of the community, and his being himself; his desire to know and be known as a person. His belief in them and their state was even cited as inspiration by the founder of the Rapson Tyre Factory. Tasmanians also came to value Sir James' sheer interest in their circumstances, and his energy and eagerness to learn what life was like for all ordinary people, no matter where in the State they lived. An urban man in a largely rural state, not only did he attend and pay attention at agricultural fairs, but he studied breeding and even began competing, precisely so that as in England farmers had the incentive of beating their King in competition, so also Tasmanians would have an additional motive to perfect their breeds and thus raise quality. He bred poultry, Ayrshire cattle, and Airedale dogs, and even won 2nd prize at his first show, for a 16-month old Gloucester Old Spot pig.

People noticed when Sir James attended events to which they had invited him, especially when he was not fully well or fit. They listened with approval when he explained his reasons for past political decisions, such as his rejection of Lloyd George's National Health Insurance Bill, and admitted to subsequently regretting those actions, and to changing his mind on the issues. Above all, they cannot fail to have been buoyed by, and to have appreciated, his glowing and passionate enthusiasm for all that Tasmania had to offer, as he rejoiced in their successes and constantly conveyed his sense of privilege at living among them. Before Sir James had been present six months, the Bishop of Tasmania was already able to comment on his "identifying himself in such a splendid way with the interests of the community." By 1927, toasts in his honour were able to make such statements as "there had been no Governor who had endeared himself more to the people than Sir James O'Grady," and "no man had got among the people more, and learnt their problems and helped them in their solution."

Beyond all these personal causes, a wide variety of sources suggest that a great deal of popularity also attached itself to the figure of Sir James' daughter Margaret. Faced with a largely unexpected role of long-term first lady of the State, she bravely stepped into public duties. Soon she was organising parties, learning to give speeches, opening fairs, and adding a flash of youth and charm to social life at Government House. From the first, she and her sister Mary were lauded as "natural, healthy, and pretty British women." Her love of dancing, tennis and keen uptake of golf all helped her make friends and contacts in Hobart, and she was soon involved in the work of the Girl Guides and the bush-nursing movement, giving a confident interview on these subjects to the Sydney *Sun* in March 1925. By June Margaret was opening her first fair, at Moonah, and indeed she seems to have made church fairs and events at all-girls' schools a speciality as time progressed.

Departure

Whatever the reasons, Sir James' popularity was such that in May 1929 it was announced that the King had extended his term of office for an additional year, to conclude in December 1930. At that time, the State finances were again tight, leading the State Government under Premier JC McPhee to request the Dominion Secretary to defer the appointment of a new Governor, whose expenses the State could ill afford. However, there was no shortage of appreciation for the departing man. As the date for departure drew closer, every organisation and event with which Sir James had been closely associated threw farewell balls and dinners in his honour. The dinner given on 15th December by the Commercial Travellers' Association in Launceston featured a special guest appearance from former Premier JA Lyons, now Federal Treasurer in Canberra. Lyons paid tribute to Sir James, calling him "Tasmania's best friend," who had "played the game" with a Nationalist government as well as a Labour one, in full accord with the example of His Majesty the King."

For his part, Sir James wrote a farewell letter to the people of Tasmania, which continued the same themes as his conversation among them. Referring to his six years in "this lovely island State" as "the most useful period of service that I have yet spent in my public life," he praised the people's kindness, responsiveness, and loyalty to the Union Flag. He urged them keep their forebears' "sacred traditions" and to face the future and its problems with courage, intelligence, enthusiasm, and "the radiant light of community spirit and fellowship."

The family's departure came in stages. They left Government House, their home of six years, for the last time on 22nd December 1930, travelling as far as Launceston. The following day, the last formal day of Sir James' extended term of office, saw them wave goodbye to Tasmania as their ship left the same harbour at which they had arrived in 1924. It was the beginning of a long journey home, via Cape Town, which would see the O'Grady family reunited at last, on the platform of London's Waterloo Station, on 9th April 1931.

On the day of his departure, the Hobart *Mercury* ran the following article under the heading "The Departure of the Governor," which serves us well as a summary of Sir James' work during this period of his life:

In leaving Tasmania to-day, after six years of his exalted office, His Excellency the Governor has the satisfaction of feeling no doubt whatever of his place in the hearts of the people from one end of the State to the other. Sir James O'Grady has not conquered this universal esteem-we might without exaggerating say affection-without effort, or it would be less to his credit! ... Sir James came here assured of a warm welcome as the King's personal representative, yet not without certain handicaps which need not now be recalled. What he did, and very wisely, was to set to work from the moment of his arrival to create his own popularity. A smaller man would have shrunk from making himself, as he would have thought, sometimes "too cheap." Not so Sir James O'Grady, who has himself admitted, and glories in the fact, that he has tried to learn and to understand the true circumstances of people of all sorts and conditions and endeavoured to ingratiate himself with all. For a long time he has been busily occupied in farewells in different parts of the country; and there is no quarter in which his personal popularity has not been demonstrated. His only rival, perhaps, is his own daughter. What we have chiefly liked in him is his constant endeavour to afford to all and sundry, from his store of wisdom, knowledge and experience garnered by a large and a keen mind from many parts of the world of affairs, the benefit of constructive hint, advice or caution such as he deemed likely to be of service ... It is his Excellency's more than pardonable' boast that he has sought to understand difficulties and get the "hang," as the saying is, of people's problems, always with the object of making practical, suggestions of a helpful nature. And it is to his credit that he has not made the mistake some Governors make of confusing a community of the highest democratic rank – if we may use that paradoxical expression – with those where a Governor is called upon to impress quite ignorant people, hardly emerged from savagery, with the awful dignity of Authority ... It is unnecessary to say that Tasmanians wish His Excellency "A Merry Christmas", and a long career of prosperity wherever his fortunes next lead him.

Fig 1 *Sailing: Sir James O'Grady on board the Orient liner* Orama *bound for Tasmania to take up his post as Governor, with his daughters Margaret O'Grady, on the left, and Mary (Molly), Mrs Kerr Cameron, and her children John and Mary. (O'Grady archives.)*

Fig 2 *With his daughter, Margaret, and grandson (his secretary and valet are also with him). (Photograph by London News LNA)*

Fig 3 *Alighting at Government House, Hobart (O'Grady archives)*

Fig 4 *Arriving at the Town Hall, Hobart (O'Grady archives)*

To His Excellency

Sir James O'Grady

K.C.M.G. ,

Governor of the State of Tasmania and its Dependencies in the Commonwealth
of Australia

MAY IT PLEASE YOUR EXCELLENCY,

WE, the Bishop, the Clergy, and the Laity of the Church of England, in the Diocese of Tasmania, affirming our loyalty to the Throne and person of our Sovereign Lord King George V., desire to offer to your Excellency a hearty and earnest welcome as you enter on the high office as Representative of His Majesty the King in this State.

Your wide experience of Public Affairs assures us that you will be able to appreciate the conditions of our life here in Tasmania.

We pray that your Excellency may have wisdom and strength for the discharge of your responsible duties, and that the blessing of Almighty God may rest upon you, Lady O'Grady—whom we hope soon to welcome to Tasmania fully restored in health—and the other members of your family.

Signed on behalf of the Bishop, the Clergy, and the Laity of the Church of England in the Diocese of Tasmania.

December, 1924.

Fig 5 Charter of welcome from the Bishop, the Clergy and the Laity of the Church of England in the diocese of Tasmania (O'Grady archives)

Fig 6 *Government House, Hobart*
(photograph supplied by the Southern Cross Assurance Co.)

Fig 7 *H.E. and Margaret with W.M. Woodsfull, Captain of*
Australian Test Cricket Team. (Photo by W. Fellowes, Hobart)

Fig 8 *Government House. Lord Stradbroke, Miss O'Grady, James O'Grady.*
(O'Grady archives)

Fig 9 *Interstate women graduates at Government House.*
(Photo by W. Fellowes, Hobart)

Fig 10 *H.E. welcoming HRH the Duke of York on board HMS* Renown.
(O'Grady archives)

Fig 11 *The Duke and Duchess of York opening the Federal Parliament of Australia in Canberra. Governor O'Grady is on the right. (Photo* Central Press, *London)*

Fig 12 *The Governor and Miss O'Grady with HRH the Duke and Duchess of York, et al, on the steps of Government House. (O'Grady archives)*

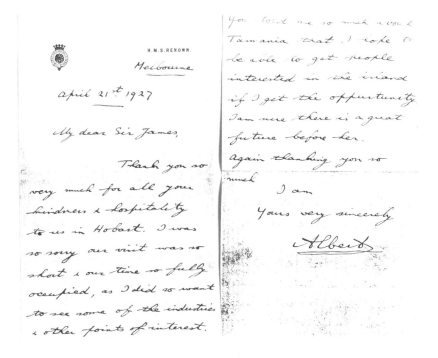

Fig 13 *Thank you letter from the Duke of York (a similar letter was received from the Duchess). (O'Grady archives)*

February 3, 1926.   ILLUSTRATED TASMANIAN MAIL   A

PARTY AT GOVERNMENT HOUSE.

Colonel Watson, Lieutenant Liggett, R.N. (A.D.C. Lord Stonehaven), Captain Bennett (A.D.C. Sir James O'Grady). Sitting (left to right): Lady Stonehaven, His (?) Vice-regal party receiving the guests. (4) and (8) Afternoon tea on the lawns. (5), (6), and (7) Some of the guests.   1, 2, 4, 8, D.I.C.; 3, 5, 6, 7, Lazern.

Fig 14 *Vice Regal party greeting guests at a gathering at Government House.*
(Illustrated Tasmania Mail)

Fig 15 *Municipal Conference. Delegates entertained at Government House.*
(O'Grady archives)

In 1933 O'Grady was delighted to receive the following letter and photograph:

Fig 16 *O'Grady Falls, Mountain Park, Hobart*

TOWN HALL,
HOBART.

TASMANIA,

4th December, 1933

His Excellency,
    Sir James O'Grady,
        Governor,
        FALKLAND ISLANDS.

Dear Sir James,

                    Mr. E.A. Stacey of Hobart, has assumed
the responsibility of delivering this letter to you personally.
Accompanying it is a photograph of "O'Grady Falls", Mount
Wellington Park, which Falls of course, are named after your
good self, and are very beautiful as will be seen from the
photograph.

                    It was intended just before you left Tasmania
on the completion of your Governorship, to ask you to pay a
visit to these Falls, and to participate in a little ceremony,
but circumstances prevented this idea being carried out.

                    Your name is permanently inscribed in our
City's history, and as long as it lasts, so will the name of
O'Grady Falls last.

                    I have read with anxiety the various accounts
which were despatched to Tasmania of your recent serious illness,
and the later reassuring news that you have effected a complete
recovery. This has been the source of great satisfaction to us all

                    We still, and will, I am sure, retain a very
happy recollection of your period of office in Tasmania, and you
will be pleased to know that in Hobart and other parts, they all
speak in affectionate terms of yourself and daughter, whose
marriage we notice took place recently.

                    I trust that you will be long spared to carry
on the important work at Falkland Islands; work which I am assured
by those in Authority, will be of very great importance to the
British Empire.

                    With kind regards,
                        I am,
                            Yours sincerely,

Fig 17 *and accompanying letter*

Launceston
'Examiner'
2/10/31

GOVERNMENT BY DICTATORSHIP

To the Editor

Sir,—Do we receive a quid pro quo for the immense outlay by 200,000 people for government by Parliament? I would bet my last ducat that any schoolboy of 14 would answer "No." Why, then, do we suffer it? Apathy, deadly apathy!

Some eighteen months before Sir James O'Grady left Tasmania, and when the financial position of the state and the unit in the community was not nearly so acute, I wrote a letter to "The Examiner" suggesting (in the modest manner which is my wont) that the question of a benevolent dictator in place of the cumbersome, effete, and go-slow Parliament be seriously taken into front rank thought, and named Sir James O'Grady as a nominee for the job. He had every qualification as I saw it; was a finished diplomat, had a world knowledge of men and things, had a brain capacity far above the ordinary successful business man; had a charm of manner and deportment; and was imbued with the best thought on the highest Christian ethics, was deeply spiritual, and his sense of honour was beyond the reach of barter. But my voice was as one crying in the wilderness, and the opportunity, like the water for the mill-wheel, glided by.

Surely now is the time, if ever, when such a project is worth consideration. We are snowed in by taxation, national, state, municipal, boards, trusts, and committees and commissions. Each takes its toll, and surely we have reached the breaking point.

Now, I will make my proposition, and if it receives the same treatment as the previous one, viz., contempt by silence, I will return no more to the attack, but allow the community to wallow in its own gravy of taxation. But the trouble is, I have to wallow with them. But, stay; I remember one individual of my acquaintance in a hurried amble by murmured to me, speaking of my first epistle on the subject, that "it was a jolly good letter, old man." So far so good.

To the crux of the job. I suggest the formation of a small committee, which will appoint officers and a secretary, who will circularise bodies such as the heads of churches, Chambers of Commerce and Manufacture, 50,000 League, Rotary Club, all political organisations, trade unions, City Council, etc., to meet and discuss the matter in all its bearings, and come to a decision whether to

"Bear those ills we have,
Or fly to others we know not of."

In conclusion, should something be done on the lines suggested, and a benevolent dictator, with strong Christian ideals, be ultimately granted power, I will venture to give a synopsis of events leading up to that result:—Preliminary meeting of committee; the Government indulges in loud chuckle. Large committee formed; Government sneers. Committee makes good headway; Government still laughs, but feebler. Movement extends to the country; Government sits up and takes notice. Movement takes hold of all sections of the community; Government alarmed. Proclamation of appointment of dictator. Dictator passes in, Government passes out, unwept, unhonoured, and unsung. Currand contentment.—Yours, etc.,
A. STUART.

Fig 18 *Government by dictatorship*

PART VI

THE FALKLAND ISLANDS

Previously published in *The Dictionary of Falklands Biography,* edited and published by David Tatham

Fig 1 *Sir James O'Grady with some of his grandchildren in England before leaving for the Falkland Islands, 1931 From left to right: The author, Patricia, James, Pauline, Michael, Anthony (none too pleased when called in from play!)*

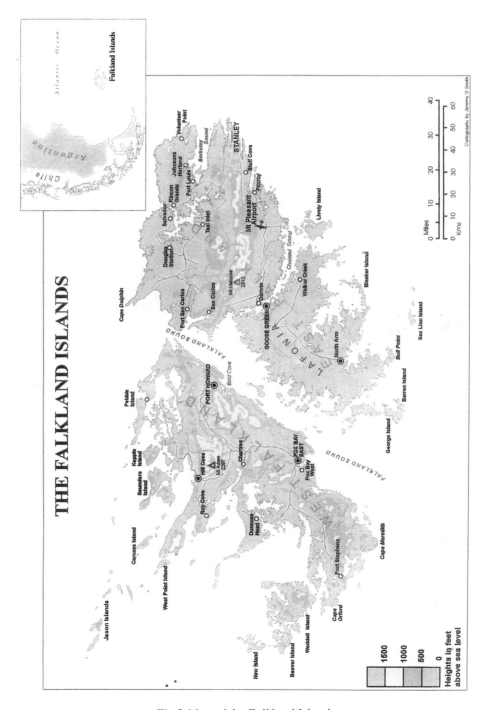

Fig 2 *Map of the Falkland Islands*

In the spring of 1931, after only one month at home since his return from Tasmania, Sir James O'Grady accepted the appointment of Governor and Commander in Chief of the Falkland Islands and Dependencies.

In an article in the News Chronicle of 29th April, he gave his reasons for accepting, namely "a love of the work of Colonial administration. When I think of the fine work being done in all parts of the world by handfuls of our men, I cannot bear the thought of settling down and doing nothing. It is not in my make up to do so."

Sir James sailed in the *Asturias* (*see* Fig 3) to Montevideo and thence in the SS *Falkland* to Stanley, but due to heavy seas and the light tonnage of the vessel (350 tons), he arrived on Saturday 20th June, four days late, but reported proudly in a letter to His Majesty King George V that he never missed a meal during the voyage and that he landed in full regalia.

Before disembarking, the Governor thanked Captain Evans and the ship's company for their good care of him during the voyage.

The weather was fine and, according to *The Penguin* (the local newspaper), Stanley turned out in full force to give him a warm welcome, flags flying everywhere.

Accompanied by the Colonel Secretary The Hon. J.M. Ellis, and the private Secretary G.R.L. Brown, and following the formalities of introduction and inspection of the Guard of Honour, the Governor proceeded to the Council Chamber (*see* Fig 4) to take the customary oath on assumption of the administration of government.

He then gave the following address:

> "Mr Ellis, Ladies and Gentlemen: I have come a long way from home in order that I may live among you for a period of years and, I hope, in order that I may enter into your activities and share with you, in a neighbourly way, what-ever difficulties there are in front of you. In addition to that I have only one purpose in view and that is to fulfil the terms of the Commission handed to me by His Majesty the King, in fairness, with no preconceived notions, no predilections, with an open ear and mind to listen to what you are doing, to

what you say and, let me repeat, to do what I can to help you.

"I counted the six years I spent as Governor of Tasmania six of the most useful years of my public life. I hope that, when I leave you, I shall be able to say the same with added experience. I have been Governor, now I have just taken the Oath for the Falkland Islands, at the two furthermost parts of the Empire.

"Indeed they are the outposts of the Empire. I have always considered outposts as, in a sense, some of the most important positions in the geography of the Empire. It is the outposts which need constant attention and, above all, which need loyal people.

"As for your loyalty, I have already had an expression of that and evidence of it in the fact of your coming and giving me this kindly welcome to-day. I had the same evidence in Tasmania.

"His Majesty the King has requested me to inform you of his kind interest in you. That may seem a rather far fetched idea, but most of us follow His Majesty in that respect. We consider this Empire of ours a natural living reality. It is a body politic. It is just as real and just as living as my body is real and living. It is a personality: an entity, representative of our characters and all we stand for. Down in this far away Island in the Southern Atlantic the people of the Falklands have got just those same faculties and qualities that our forefathers had who went abroad for adventure and found it.

"This entity known as the British Empire – it is not a manufactured thing. Indeed, if I were to describe it in simple terms we all understand, it is just like the paragraph in 'Uncle Tom's Cabin' when Topsy was asked where she was born and said 'I wasn't born, Massa, I just grow'd.'

"That simple illustration brings home what I mean by saying it is a real and living thing, and speaking with thirty-five years of active public life, the longer I live the prouder I am to be British.

"Mind you, I don't want to disparage any other man's nationality. I love all men for their patriotism which means a simple love of one's country. You are here in the Falklands and I want you to love the Falklands. To many of you it is your Homeland of the Empire. The more you love it the greater will be your love for the Empire of which it forms a part.

"I shall have opportunities, Ladies and Gentlemen, to speak to you about that idea I have just expressed. In the meantime, I want to say it is very kind of you to come here to-day. Well, I brought you the King's weather and don't forget that.

"I have enjoyed the experience and I hope you have too and that we shall all pull together during the time I am with you. If you want success you must have team work. Let there be no mistake about that. And I am happy to be one of the team with you with due regard, naturally, to the position I hold as the representative of His Majesty the King.

"Thank you very much for coming along to welcome me."

At the conclusion of the ceremonies, His Excellency left for Government House (*see* Figs 5 & 6).

Settling into his new home must have been a lonely time, having no member of his family with him. His daughter Margaret, who had been with him in Tasmania, offered to accompany him but Sir James declined, telling her "it's no place for a woman".

It would appear he didn't even have a dog for company whereas there was always one in evidence in Tasmania.

Fig 3 *H.E. aboard the* Asturias *crossing the Equator, spring 1931*

Fig 4 *Arriving at Parliament House, Stanley,*
after disembarking from the SS Falkland
on Saturday 20th June, 1931

Fig 5 *Government House, Stanley, in 1931.*
(Courtesy of Falkland Islands Government Archives)

Fig 6 *The drawing room at Government House in the 1930s.*
(Courtesy of Falkland Islands Government Archives)

Fig 7 *H.E. leaving Government House with the Commodore for the Saluting Base*

Fig 8 *The Hon. J.M. Ellis (on the left) with H.E. at Government House*

Fig 9 *The SS* Lafonia

Fig 10 *Taking the passengers ashore for the tribute*

Fig 11 *H.E. speaking to the assembly by the tombstome commemorating Matthew Brisbane*

Fig 12 *Laying the foundation stone for the swimming pool*

Fig 13 *One of the silver boxes presented by the City of Bristol*

Fig 14 *Some of the locals*

Leaving the homestead to return to the 'steamer'

With some friends

Having a picnic
Fig 16

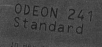

ontinued his report to the King, "The sheep farmers and
es are a fine lot of men. Their lonely life makes mem
king talk, but when one gets them to 'thaw out' their
about their work and domestic affairs is indeed interesting.
en are educated by travelling teachers, employed by the
t, and the respect in which these teachers are held by the
feature that is wholly blessed. I came away from these folks
an, I am certain, than before I met them. They were kind
say that my talk was helpful and pressed that I should make
frequent."

s reported in 'The Penguin' that, for his tour of farm stations in
y Sound and Salvador Waters, H. E. was accompanied by the
Hon. L. W. H. Young, Manager of the Falkland Islands Company and
the Hon. G. Roberts, Director of Public Works.

For the visit to the West Falklands by the SS *Lafonia* (Fig 9) he was
accompanied by the Colonial Secretary.

Towards the end of February, Sir James received the sad news that
his son-in-law, Sidney Martin, had been killed in a car crash, ending,
prematurely, his career as a noted 'black and white artist' and cartoonist,
and leaving his widow, Sir James' second daughter Norah, and two
young children (Michael and Diana).

His Excellency must have felt very far from home and from his
family at this time.

There are no reports of official activities by the Governor until
December 1932. He will, however, have been fully occupied planning
for the Islands' Centenary in 1933.

We know that, during this time, he requested the gift of a cup for
the races from His Majesty the King (*see* appendix I) and, from the
Admiralty, a visit from a warship for the celebrations.

Before the year's ending, H. E. attended the Bazaar held by St.
Mary's Roman Catholic Mission to raise funds for the Mission School.
He spoke appreciatively of the good will between the different Christian
Missions and, as a member of the Roman Catholic Church, of the heroic
work being done by Father Migone and the Sisters for the school and
the work of the Mission.

The last report for 1932 was that the Governor was due to leave Stanley on 22nd December for a week's round trip of the Islands aboard the SS *Lafonia* accompanied by the Colonial Secretary.

Where, we wonder, did H. E. enjoy the Christmas festivities? On board the *Lafonia* or at one of the farmsteads?

The celebration of the Falklands Centenary in 1933 began with a tribute to the memory of Matthew Brisbane, Britain's first appointed Governor of the Islands.

The celebrations continued with a week of festivities described by the Governor in a letter to his daughter Mary (Molly):

"... Curiously enough we had the weather of the century – a week of glorious, warm sunshine.

We had the H.M.S. Durban in, also Discovery II, the latter is the research ship that has, for some time, been investigating sea life and currents.

The proceedings opened with a review, under arms, on the large paddock facing Government House. I took the salute in full uniform, afterwards attending service at the Cathedral.

Throughout the week, there was horse racing, sports, dancing in the Town Hall every night and a fine display of fireworks. Ninety percent of the total population of the colony were in Stanley for the celebrations.

Everything went off without a hitch and everybody, particularly the children, enjoyed themselves immensely.

I am persuading the folks to have a "do" every 3 years so that the feeling of mutual regard generated shall be perpetuated. The sheep farmers and their shepherds rarely come in to Stanley, therefore they and the town people are complete strangers. It will be to the good of the colony if they meet every 3 years and have a week of festivities."

The Governor laid the foundation stone for a swimming pool (Fig 12). He wrote in a letter to Sir Clive Wigram private secretary to H. M. King George V:

> "Our swimming pool, I am afraid, will not be built yet owing to the lack of finances. However it is a beginning and such a swimming pool is a very great necessity here as there are only about fifteen men and boys in the whole colony who can really swim. I am hoping that some of the better-to-do people will help me with the financing of this project."

His letter continues:

> "The gracious message of the King was enthusiastically received. It made all of us feel that in this far outpost of Empire we were remembered still. Quite a number of the sheep farmers speaking of the King's message mentioned how intimate it was and felt that the King had actually sent his words to them direct."

Here His Excellency digressed to speak of the problem caused by Argentina's claim to the Sovereignty of the Falkland Islands, then continued:

> "Going back to the Centenary celebrations. I must say that I was agreeably surprised at the behaviour of the men from the camp, having regard to the lonely life they lead and to the fact that many of them had never been in Stanley before, and I took care at the final function on the Saturday night to express publicly my sincere thanks for their behaviour through the week. Of course a few of them quite naturally partook rather freely of the strong – very strong – beer we import and being myself naturally of a cautious turn of mind – you may not believe that – I had about twelve special constables sworn in but gave them definite instructions

that they were to arrest no man, no matter what his style of walking might be at the moment, but instead they were to take him to his diggings and get him put to bed. So there were no arrests and no gaoling."

Perhaps the celebrations were appropriately concluded with a gift to the Colony from the City of Bristol of a silver smoking set (Fig 13) for use at Government House.

The following letter to His Excellency was published in 'The Penguin' on 24th February 1933:

Dear Sir James,

On behalf of Bristol citizens, it is my pleasure as Lord Mayor of the city, to convey to the Colony of which you are the Governor greetings and congratulations upon the occasion of its Centenary Celebrations.

As a tangible expression of our goodwill, we are forwarding by insured parcels post and by the present outgoing mail, a silver Smoking Set for use at Government House, Port Stanley. This consists of a cigar box, cigarette box and a pair of lighters, all made by Bristol craftsmen in distinctive style. The inscriptions emphasise the occasion of the Centenary and also record your own Governorship of the Colony.

This presentation Set has been subscribed to by many local bodies and societies and by many interested individuals including present day City Councillors of all parties. I hope that it will prove useful both to yourself and to your successors at Government House.

Bristol values the links that exist between herself and the Empire's most southern Colony. The remains of a famous Bristol-built ship lie in Port Stanley Harbour and both the Lord Bishop of the Falklands and yourself as Governor and Commander-in-Chief have most intimate connections with Bristol. The personal greetings which this letter conveys to yourself extend also to the Lord Bishop whom so many

Bristolians will remember with great affection.

I conclude with the hope that the Centenary Celebrations of next month will be fortunate and happy and with the assurance that the small commemorative gift we are sending expresses the real interest and goodwill of the many citizens of Bristol concerned with it.

I am, dear Sir James,

Yours sincerely,

Sd. Thos. J. Woso,

Lord Mayor.

On each of the gift boxes the Arms of Bristol City and the Falklands appear in enamel and the City Arms are also engraved on the swing lighters which, together with the feet of each box, are carved in the form of dolphins by one of the City's oldest craftsmen.

"The story of the dolphin" His Excellency explained to a representative of the 'Penguin' yesterday "goes back to the days of the Tudors when Edward Colston, one of the old merchant venturers from the city of Bristol, with his own fleet of sailing ship, roamed the seas. Coming home from one of his voyages the vessel on which he happened to be on board struck a rock and knocked a hole in her bottom. The old man was deeply religious and he went down on his hands and knees and prayed for a miracle. The miracle happened for a dolphin stuck its head in the hole and plugged the leak so enabling the ship to get back to Bristol. When they beached her they found the remains of the dolphin firmly fixed where the rock had penetrated the hull.

"So rose into being the Dolphin Society the dinners of which, pre-war, were the second greatest functions in the Kingdom from the political point of view. They were second to the Guild Hall Dinners where the Prime Minister and other statesmen declared their policy, and the Ministers used to visit the Dolphin Society's dinner to speak.

"Edward Colston, like many other merchant venturers of his days, was a great benefactor to the city of Bristol. In addition to the Dolphin Society, he founded the Colston School - a famous school in the city - where the boys still wear a long robe, yellow stockings, brogue shoes and breeches while, with other merchant venturers, he also founded the Red Maids School."

On 3 June, the King's Birthday was commemorated by a grand parade of the Defence Force, the Sea Rovers, Boy Scouts and Girl Guides, Wolf Cubs and Brownies. It was held on the Government House paddock and was followed by a Review of the Defence Force with His Excellency taking the Salute. The Defence Force was headed by the brass band recently formed.

At the conclusion of the Parade the Governor and his staff visited the Defence Force Headquarters where His Majesty's health was drunk.

Undoubtedly at this time of his Governorship, Argentina's claim to the sovereignty of the Falkland Islands caused some difficulties for the islanders and some irritation to himself.

As he reported to Sir Clive Wigram:

> "... For instance they (i.e. the Government of Argentina) paid us some £627 owing as the result of some wireless business. The arrangements for payment were made in the ordinary way through our Ambassador in the Argentine but they took care when remitting the money to declare that in so doing they in no sense invalidated their 'Sovereign Rights'. Also, they will not recognise our passports and insist upon our people when they arrive in the Argentine, taking out another passport. There are some other acts of theirs that while irritating, need not be commented upon but the last of their pretensions – the matter of our Centenary Stamps – seems to be about the limit Our stamps are declared to be invalid when the Falkland Islands' people write to their friends in the Argentine; they are surcharged and a fine is imposed before delivery can be effected. Further than that,

they have written to the International Postal Bureau at Berne informing them that in view of Argentina's 'Sovereign Rights' they are to take notice that the Falkland Islands stamps are invalid. Incidentally, from the philatelists' point of view the stamps will become much more valuable as a result of this extraordinary attitude of the Argentine.

I will take care that the King shall receive a set if there are any new issues."

It was announced on 1st July 1933 that the Governor was indisposed and had gone in to Hospital.

This was followed by His Excellency's message to the people of the Colony (6th July 1933):

"Circumstances compel me to be absent from you for a while and I would like you to take my departure on sick leave as just' Au Revoir' with my grateful thanks for all your kindnesses, hospitality and courtesy since I came to you as Governor, directly representing His Majesty the King.

I am sure you will understand me when I say that my thanks are in a special sense due to Dr. Innes Moir, Dr. Glyn Edmunds and the Staff of the Hospital for their care and attention to me during the time of early sickness.

I am hoping to be back with you again recovered in health sufficiently to help in carrying through a number of projects that I have in mind leading to more efficient government and increase of the welfare of the people of the Colony."

It was then reported that the Governor had departed on Saturday 8th July in the s.s. 'Lafonia' bound for Montevideo and thence for England. H. E. was accompanied on the voyage by Dr. G. H. Edmunds and by his valet, Mr. E. Headford.

The cause of his 'indisposition' was given in the British press as blood poisoning; he had also suffered for many years from diabetes.

His Excellency returned to England for specialist treatment and bis health made some initial improvement; this was not sustained and he remained on sick leave, living with his family, until his death in a London nursing home on 10th December 1934.

Postcript. From a letter from Mrs. Jane Cameron, government Archivist, Falkland Islands.

On 7th July of 1933, the day before Governor O'Grady was due to depart for England on medical grounds, the Colonial Manager of the Falkland Islands Company, L. W. H. Young wrote in one of his despatches to the Directors in London:

> "I fear he is unlikely to return, which is to be regretted. I have always found him to reasonable (sic) and just; he had a keen perception of the difficulties of the farmers, but has been greatly handicapped during his administration by the legacies left him by his predecessor and by unemployment."

The passage is particularly interesting in view of the fact that traditionally Governors and Falkland Islands Company Managers were at loggerheads, so it seems that Governor O'Grady managed to overcome this long-standing convention.

PRIVY PURSE OFFICE,
BUCKINGHAM PALACE, S.W.

3rd October 1932.

Dear Sir James O'Grady,

     The King, who has seen your letter to Wigram, has been speaking to me about the possibility of his giving a Cup for the Falkland Islands Centenary. I have, however, explained to His Majesty that so many requests from different parts of the British Empire for Cups are sent to him every year, that it has not been found possible to make any satisfactory selection of Colonies to which Cups should be sent; the only exception being the larger Dominions. The King therefore wishes me to explain this to you, and at the same time to express His Majesty's regret that he is unable to do what you ask.

Yours sincerely,

Keeper of the Privy Purse.

His Excellency,
    Sir James O'Grady, K.C.M.G.
        Government House,
            Falkland Islands.

For his journey home on sick leave, the Governor was required to make a passport for himself!

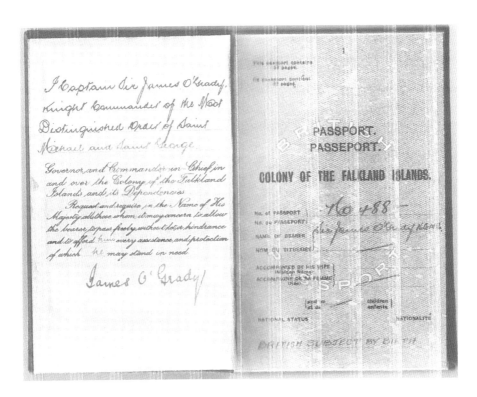

After his death, the family received many letters of condolence, including one from King George V and Queen Mary.

The most poignant was from Ben Tillet:

NATIONAL TRADE UNION CLUB
LIMITED

President:
A. G. WALKDEN
General Secretary, Railway Clerks' Association

Hon. Treasurer:
GEORGE HICKS, M.P.
Amalgamated Union of Building Trade Workers and President National Federation of Labour Clubs

Chairman:
BEN TILLETT
Transport and General Workers' Union

Hon. Secretary:
C. J. KEBBELL
National Union of Commercial Travellers

Telephones: HOLBORN 4166 4167 2 lines

Secretary-Manager:
W. ARTHUR PEACOCK
National Union of Journalists

Bankers:
BARCLAYS BANK, British Museum Branch

24/28 New Oxford Street
London, W.C.1

December 15th 1924.

To Michael O' Grady & Sisters.

My dear Bonnies:
I still feel the numbness of the ceremony giving you dear Father back to Mother-Earth. The abrupt leaving of the Reverend Father, shocked me; but his rendering of the funeral ritual was kindly & profound.
'It was all impressive in beauty & thought; then it carried with it, the soul of your brave father-whose life had been glorious in service to the Empire and the World alike.
He was Bristol born like unto myself, and all his childhood belonged to the quays and harbour of Bristol, he knew ship. and cargoes; the loadings and the unloadings, the repairs & preparations for voyages abroad again.
His life was romantic and gallant in service & duty- as a Raleigh; or, even a Drake-in venture and the Command of the Colony and Dominions alike, which he honoured with grace & an Intellectual power comparable to the best ever given to the wider Empire duties, of our greatest Statesmen.
Our far flung Imperialism adjudicated to him the responsibility of administering the Falkland Islands, the toughest outpost of the Empire and the "Spear head" of the Pacific Ocean, where relationships of the Empire as a whole may be challenged & questioned as to power & authority, by the pacific and eastern world.
It's wind-bound and storm-bound islets make the Falklands a raging riot of storms and gales of violent power & destructive potentiality.
Devotion counts the greater when a great Governor endures with fortitude the terrific demands upon his strength & stamina; your dear Father gave a wonderful gift of manhood, when he served with fidelity & courage a post, the outpost of his Imperial-Majesty.
He was your Father, he gave nobility to his dear Family whom he loved; your Mother who braved and served your lives in the agony of a great affliction; with years of torture.
Such a Father, such a Mother endured their crucifixin as they lived and loved and nursed you all into being and life.
God bless you all, give you also all that health & happiness denied in too many ways to your glorious parents.
As the life Comrades of your parents and as your loving friend I bid you be of good cheer.

And perhaps the most interesting was from the Association of Officers of Taxes from which I quote:

"Years ago, when this Association was known as the Association of Tax Clerks, and did not number as many hundreds as it now numbers thousands, Sir James rendered conspicuous services to our members. During the period when he was M.P. for Leeds from 1966 onwards, he took a very keen interest indeed in the claim which was made by the Clerks to Surveyors of Taxes that they should be put on a permanent(sic) and pensionable footing in the Civil Service.

Sir James did exceedingly good work on behalf of the Association of that day, and was instrumental in bringing before two successive Chancellors of the Exchequer the unsatisfactory conditions under which these unestablished Public Servants were working.

It was undoubtedly through Sir James's efforts that the Clerks first secured establishment in the Civil Service in 1908, a process which was finally completed in 1914.

Those of our members who were serving at that time have never forgotten the help they received from the late Sir James, and followed with keen interest his subsequent career."

BIBLIOGRAPHY

Prologue
The Climate of Treason by Andrew Boyle (Hutchinson of London)

Part I Forbears and Early Life
Oxford Dictionary of National Biography, article by D.E.Martin (Oxford University Press 2004–6)
Dictionary of Labour Biography Volume III Joyce M. Bellamy, Senior Research Officer University of Hull and John Saville Professor of Economic and Social History University of Hull. Deakin University Library 13th July 1983.

Part II Political Life
Men who made Labour by Diane Hayter and Alan Hayworth, article by Hilary Benn MP for Leeds Central (Taylor Francis Group)

Part IV Russia
Chapter I: Revolution
Witnesses of the Revolution by Harvey Pitcher(John Murray Ltd)
'Report to the War Cabinet on the visit of the Labour Delegation to Russia', April to May 1917 by Lieutenant W.S.Sanders (National Archives)
The File on the Tsar by Anthony Summers and Tom Mangold (Victor Gollancz Ltd)
A Lifelong Passion by Andrei Maylunas & Sergei Mironenko (Wiedenfeld & Nicolson, London)

Chapter II: Exchange of Prisoners
Between the Revolution and the West by Hugh Phillips (Westview Press, Oxford)
The Story of ST 25 by Paul Dukes (Wyman and Sons Ltd)

Baltic Episode by Capt Augustus Agar VC (Conway Maratime Express)

Letter to King George V from Grand Duchess Cyril of Russia (National Archives)

Report to Earl Curzon on the work of the Delegation of the Exchange of the Prisoners of War and Civilian Nationals by James O'Grady (National Archives)

Chapter III: Famine

Letter dated April 12th 1922 from E.G.Wilton of the British Legation in Riga to Lord Curzon, then British Foreign Secretary. (National Archives)

Letter from International Federation of Trade Unions to James O'Grady (O'Grady Archives)

Soviet Russia, The Road to Famine from the Pageant of the Years by Sir Philip Gibbs (Heinemann)

Conclusion

Letter from the British Legation in Riga to the Foreign Office in London (National Archives)

Article on the Zinoviev letter from the *Crown Jewels* by Nigel West and Oleg Tsarev

Letter to O'Grady from Lord Stamfordham, Private Secretary to King George V (O'Grady Archives)

Entr'actes

Excerpt from the *London Evening Standard* March 11, 1924 page 6 'A Londoner's Diary' para 4

Part V Tasmania

The main source for this section has been the O'Grady family archives, particularly in the form of collected newspaper cuttings from the time, including but not limited to the following titles:- *The Burnie Advocate*, the Launceston *Daily Telegraph* and *Examiner*, the Hobart *Mercury*, the *Illustrated Tasmanian Mail* and the *Melbourne Argus*.

Additional information has been drawn from the National Library of Australia digitised newspaper pages.

Part VI The Falkland Islands

Sir James O'Grady's letter to H.M. King George V and his secretary Sir Clive Wigram (Royal Archives, Windsor Castle, RN/PS/GV/P2348/10

APPENDICES

APPENDIX I

WAR CABINET MINUTES 104, MINUTE 5

Mr. Henderson stated that he had received a communication to the effect that representatives of the French Socialist Party who stood for War a Outrance were, with the authority and consent of the French Committee of Foreign Affairs, shortly arriving in England en route to Petrograd where they were going on a mission to the Russian Socialist Party, their object being to persuade that Party to do all in its power to bring the war to a satisfactory conclusion.

The War Cabinet decided that Mr. Henderson should use his influence to secure that a suitably composed British Labour Party Delegation should accompany the French party, with the same object.

MINUTES OF THE WAR CABINET, 28TH MARCH, 1917

March 27th - With reference to War Cabinet Minutes 104, Minute 5, Mr Henderson reported that Mr. Thomas would not be able to go to Russia; he believed that Mr. Thorne and Mr. O'Grady would be willing to accompany the Delegation, and he hoped that Lt. Sanders might also be available, which the Secretary of State for War stated would be practicable.

The general view of the War Cabinet was in favour of a reliable Russian Socialist being attached to the Mission as an Interpreter, and of the addition of a more academic socalist of the type of Mr. Hyndeman.

APPENDIX II

PART IV RUSSIA – CHAPTER I – REVOLUTION

[This Document is the Pr erty of His Britannic Maje y s Government.] 282

Printed for the War Cabinet.- June 1917

SECRET.

G-150.   5

REPORTS ON THE VISIT OF THE LABOUR DELEGATION TO
RUSSIA, APRIL–MAY 1917.

I.—GENERAL REPORT.

The Military Situation.

GENERAL GOURKO put the position thus :—

"The armies under the old regime used to attack when ordered. Now the order to attack would be discussed by Soldiers Councils and either delay or refusal would follow."

The General was quite candid in explaining the reasons now given by the Councils. Under the old dispensation attacks were made, often without sufficient artillery for modern warfare, barbed wire having to be cut with "nippers" with consequent heavy losses in men. The General, of course, is a man who believes in men obeying orders no matter the consequences. But there was no doubt in our minds that he volunteered this statement as showing how difficult it was to discipline an army under the circumstances. Gourko and other Generals we met had anxieties about the new officers commissioned straight from the "ranks." Firstly, it being impossible for them to go through the schools, their lack of knowledge did not tend to make them become efficient officers. Secondly, such officers—as was natural—had strong political revolutionary ideas, and therefore the ears of the Workers' and Soldiers' Councils. It naturally followed that there was an hiatus between old and new régime officers. After visiting the armies of the North and West fronts, the former under General Russky's command, and the latter under General Gourko's, we came away with the impression that for all practical purposes, those armies could be chalked out. There seemed an utter absence of discipline in the army under Russky. Two incidents that came within our knowledge will in some degree show the measure of indiscipline. We were informed by a soldier speaking English that his comrades at that time frequently fraternised with the enemy in the front firing lines and that only the week prior to our addressing the troops, a large meeting had taken place at which a resolution was carried unanimously declaring that officers' pay, from General to subaltern must be the same as privates. The soldier declared they expected the Workmen and Soldiers' Council to see the resolution carried into effect. Another incident showing that the High Command had lost control, or were impotent in the matter of enforcing discipline, occurred at the table of General Vsouloukeidze, with whom we lunched. The private soldier, delegate from Minsk, who was with us, held a meeting of junior officers at the opposite end of table to that where the General sat. From the interpreter we gathered that the soldier was denouncing M. Miliukoff and the Provisional Government in general. He was also urging the young officers—not much urging required--to impress upon other officers, and men to stand by the instructions issued from time to time by the Workmen and Soldiers' Council. The General heard this man and looked on helplessly. We were informed food supplies of troops were bad, materials of war were lacking, horses were dying for want of fodder, transport facilities wretched, and desertions had, up to that time, taken place *en masse*. We felt the only hope for this state of things was the formation of Coalition Government with strong Minister for War. That has since happened; but these were our impressions at the time.
Too gloomy a view ought not to be taken ; for bad as the situation was, it would

                                                                          B

65

2

have been much worse had the old régime been existing. Bad as affairs were, the Coalition Government, before we left Russia, had brought about an improvement, and the improvement showed evidence of accelerating progress.

Neither should a gloomy view be taken of the reports now coming from Russia with regard to soldiers' deputies coming back from armies to Petrogrd, Moscow, Dvinsk, Minsk, and Pskov. Their reports of soldiers' determinations and the comments re same in their "journals," and the extracts from both wired to newspapers here, are simply phrases; disturbing, it is true, to us Westerners, but of less weight to Russian people. All these reports as published in newspapers at home ought to be judged in the light of those reporting the visit of M. Kerensky and M. Thomas to the troops. Similar reports and comments in our newspapers do not better the position. The effect they *do* produce is to dishearten the men at head of affairs, working at an almost super-human task. Cannot something be done similar to the action taken some time ago, when Mr. Balfour met the editors in London ?

The Political Situation.

The leaders of Workmen and Soldiers' Council are in the Coalition to press that the Allies shall issue a new note, accepting the policy of "no annexations, &c." This is a real danger spot, because unless the Allies do something in the matter, the Coalition will break up, and possibly a separate peace with Germany will become the propaganda of the Workmen and Soldiers' Council. We believe that "no annexations, &c.," are mere phrases. When asked whether Alsace-Lorraine becoming again French territory was annexation, Deputies replied "No !" When asked whether Germany should pay for material damage done in Belgium, France, Serbia, the Deputies replied "Yes !" They didn't consider that charge a contribution or indemnity. We asked if they would accept the phrases "Restitution" and "Reparation" in place of their "No annexations, &c." They replied that this seemed reasonable, but would not definitely commit themselves.

The civil population are led to believe that there is now nothing to continue the war for. They have their freedom—what more is necessary, &c. ? They are swayed in this direction by intense German propaganda, carried on right through Russia. This propaganda is not only for separate peace, but viciously anti-British. Russia is flooded with German agents and money, and their organisation and operation ranges from purchase of newspapers and flooding of workshops and armies with leaflets to paying women to stand in food queues denouncing Great Britain as responsible for shortage, high prices, and continuance of war. Not only that—and on this point there should be no doubt—German propaganda is intent upon establishing an opinion favour-able to German economic exploitation of Russia when the war is over. In this connec-tion it ought to be stated that our Consular Service in Russia is in a bad state. We have not generally men of sufficient calibre in brains, training, or experience. Perhaps this arises from the fact that salaries are wretchedly low. In an important industrial centre like Moscow we pay our consul 600*l.* per annum. Mr. Lockhart, the present consul, is a very capable man, high in the estimation of the British colony and of Russians generally. But 600*l.* a year for a man like Mr. Lockhart is in itself poor pay, to say nothing of keeping up the status of a British representative. We suggest that in every consulate of importance there should be two men, one having charge of commer-cial matters and the other carrying on the duties of the consulate as at present—the latter to be the superior officer. With great respect we urge that Russia is an Empire of great area, with a population of 180 millions, and with enormous possibilities of not only being a great market, but of developing into the greatest economic Power in the world. Its mineral, oil, and food-producing resources are practically untapped. When war is over, the struggle in exploiting these resources will, if no effort is now put forward by Great Britain, remain a matter of conquest between America and Germany, with advantages in favour of the latter.

Admittedly Russia and its part in the war is at the moment the grave concern of our Government. But the future of our relations, economic and political, ought not to be overlooked, even in the throes and travail of waging the war.

Food Prices and Wages.

Owing to the absence of organisation, people often wait in queues all day and night, and, on arriving at shop-doors, were told "Sold out." It is not correct to say that the increase of wages has inflated food prices. There were scarcely any increases

3

up to the fall of the old régime, and since then wages have not risen unreasonably. At a Putilov factory in Petrograd the wages of women under the old régime were 2·88 a day, and are now 4 roubles. True, when we left Moscow, weavers were demanding an increase from 1·50 roubles a day to 4·50. But a system existed by which employers bought food and supplied it to workers at pre-war prices. Presumably, at a wage of 4·50 workers would buy their own food. Prices of food have risen almost wholly as a result of lack of transport, lack of organisation, fall in value of rouble, and profiteering.*

JAMES O'GRADY.
WILL THORNE.
WM. STEPHEN SANDERS.

II.—Report by the Secretary to the Delegation.

The Petrograd Workmen's and Soldiers' Council.

On arrival at Petrograd on the 14th April, we got into touch immediately with the Provisional Government and the Workmen and Soldiers' Council. The Provisional Government received us most cordially, and made arrangements for us to visit the Russian front. The Workmen and Soldiers' Council Executive Committee received us at first with a certain amount of reserve, but they were quite courteous, and the discussions we held with them from time to time were carried on quite amicably. The Council is composed of soldiers' deputies elected from regiments and workmen from factories, together with delegates from various sections of the Socialist movement, the four principal being the two wings of the Social Democratic Party (who are the most doctrinaire), the Socialist Revolutionary Party, and the Labour group.

The Council's Pronouncement on the War.

The Executive Committee of the Council were eager to know the attitude of the British Labour movement towards their pronouncement on the aims of the war, and they were most anxious that we should use our influence with the British Labour party in order that the British Government might be induced to endorse the pronouncement. We pointed out to the Committee that the attitude of the British Labour and Socialist movement as a whole had been expressed in resolutions passed at the various annual conferences of the British Labour party, the Trade Union Congress, and the General Federation of Trades Unions, and that we represented the views expressed by the majority of the delegates at these conferences.

Peace Formula.

We discussed, however, at considerable length on several occasions with the Committee the terms of the pronouncement, and pointed out that the simplicity of the formula of "No annexation and no indemnities" rendered it ineffective as a statement of Allied aims. We asked whether the transference to France of Alsace-Lorraine, for instance, would be considered to be an annexation, and whether insistence upon payment from Germany for damage done in Belgium, Northern France, Poland, and elsewhere would be considered to be a demand for indemnity. We also suggested that the third clause in the pronouncement—"the right of any nationality to settle its own destiny"—would probably lead to a transference of territory and people from one Power to another, and such transference might be considered to be annexation. The Committee could not give a clear and definite interpretation of the phrase "No annexation and no indemnities"; but they agreed that transference of territories and peoples must take place, and that the damage to Belgium, Northern France, Serbia, &c., must be paid for. In reply to a direct question, the Committee repudiated the idea that they were in favour of the *status quo ante bellum*. They were, however, most anxious that the three clauses in their pronouncement should be adopted by the Allies in principle, leaving discussion of details to the Peace Conference whenever it meets. Our last meeting with the Workmen's and Soldiers' Council Executive Committee took place on the day we left Petrograd (16th May), and lasted from midnight until 4 in the morning. The main purpose of this meeting was again to endeavour to obtain

* It could not be ascertained whether scarcity of food or high prices in towns arose from the causes mentioned above, or whether there was not an actual shortage of food in the country as a whole.—W. S. S.

5

French and British delegates had taken part in their bourgeois Governments, and that they (the left wing of the Social Democratic party) believed in Russia making an immediate peace, and insisted on a social revolution throughout Europe.

I.L.P. Repudiation.

At Moscow we learnt that the I.L.P. in England had issued a repudiation of the British Delegation, stating that we did not represent the British Labour and Socialist movement. We drafted a reply to this repudiation, which appeared in a number of papers in Moscow. Following this letter, an article appeared in the organ of the Workmen and Soldiers' Committee at Petrograd explaining that we represented the views of the recognised majority of the British Labour and Socialist movement, and were therefore entitled to be received by the Labour and Socialist movement in Russia. In this connection the telegram sent to Kerensky and signed by Mr. H. M. Hyndman and others proved most useful. It should be mentioned that the repudiation of us by the I.L.P. did not appear to affect adversely our relations with the various workmen and soldiers' organisations with whom we came in contact. We were always given an opportunity to explain who and what we represented, and it was only extremists, such as Lenin, who made use of the I.L.P. resolutions and statements which appeared in English papers against us.

Visit to the Front.

From Moscow we paid a ten days' visit to the Western and Northern fronts. We addressed a number of meetings of soldiers. On some occasions the meetings comprised from 3,000 to 5,000 men. We were always received with enthusiasm, especially when we impressed upon the soldiers the necessity of defeating German militarism in order to ensure the permanence of Russian freedom. At these meetings, however, two delegates from the Soldiers' and Workmen's Committee at Minsk also spoke. One of them talked crude Marxist socialism and laid great stress on the necessity of the Allies agreeing to the terms of peace drafted by the Workmen's and Soldiers' Council at Petrograd, repeating continuously the phrase of "no annexations and no contributions." It is true that he also declared that there must be no separate peace and no fraternising with the Germans, but the impression he conveyed was that the war was practically a capitalist one, and therefore not of particular moment to the Russian democracy. We did our utmost to nullify this impression, and we think we were to a certain extent successful.

Interviews with General Gourko.

We had two interviews with General Gourko who expressed the opinion that his army would, if time could be given, get over the disorganisation caused by the revolution and settle down to steady campaigning. He pointed out, however, that there were still grave difficulties in connection with transport, leading to shortage of ammunition. There was also insufficient fodder for horses which rendered movement very difficult. We also met General Russky at his headquarters, but as he was ill we were not able to discuss the situation with him. He had, moreover, resigned on the day we visited him.

The Soldiers' Committees.

We were struck by the excellent physique of the Russian soldiers and their remarkably good spirits considering the circumstances in which they had been living during the winter. There is, however, no doubt that there are certain elements in the Soldiers' Committees who are more interested in politics and in peace than in restoring discipline on a new basis in the army. Both in the Soldiers' and Workmen's Councils and the Soldiers' Committees the Jewish element is very strong, and we could not help feeling, although none of us is an anti-Semite, that the Jewish influence has nearly always an anti-British and pacifist tendency, arising probably from the fact that the Jews in these Comittees are nearly always extreme Socialists, whose socialism is drawn almost entirely from German sources. It was the Jews who, almost invariably, brought up at our meetings questions relating to English rule in Ireland, Egypt, or India and criticised British Imperialism which they insisted was the counterpart of German Imperialism. They lost no opportunity of urging an immediate peace at almost any price.

6

Discipline in the Army.

It is difficult to express an opinion as to the state of discipline in the armies as a whole that we visited. In some places it appeared to be good and relations between officers and men quite satisfactory ; on the other hand, in some places, as for instance at Pskov, we were informed privately by the officers that the men were decidedly insubordinate. We were told by a number of officers, including Generals, that the rank and file refused to do outpost duty and this had to be done by the officers themselves. In general there was an air of slackness about all the armies, an absence of definite work which, we could not help thinking must tend to inefficiency, although we were informed that we must not judge the Russian army from the British standpoint.

The Coalition Ministry.

On our return to Petrograd the crisis which ended in the establishment of the Coalition Ministry was at its height, and it was not completely settled until after the time of our departure ; but we feel that the settlement arrived at has caused great improvement in the situation. Kerensky, whom we met, struck us as being a very sincere and able man with a powerful personality. He appears to be trusted both by the workmen and the soldiers. The other Labour and Socialist representatives who joined the Coalition have also the confidence of the people they represent, and are, with the exception perhaps of Skobelef, level-headed and sensible men. Skobelef is not an extremist, but he is nevertheless a very strong pacifist, with an almost pathetic belief that the Russian revolution will influence the German people to bring about a movement on similar lines in Germany, which will be followed by peace. He is a visionary, apparently with little experience of affairs.

The Cost of Living.

With regard to the civil population there is no doubt a strong feeling in favour of peace, owing largely to the difficulties in connection with the food supply. The cost of living has gone up tremendously in the towns; for instance, in Moscow careful examination of prices, based on statistics supplied by a local hospital, showed that the cost of living had increased in that town 400 per cent. since the beginning of the war. We were informed by some people that there was plenty of food in the country, but the difficulties of transport caused a lack of supply in the towns. Other persons assured us that the stock of food in the country was, unfortunately, very low ; but we had no means of finding out the truth of either of these statements. The cost of living has also been artificially inflated by increases in wages and by the presence in the towns of large numbers of well-to-do persons, who previously lived in the districts now occupied by the enemy.

Labour Unrest.

Unrest, caused largely by high prices coupled with disclosed high profits, appeared to be very rife in the factories in the Moscow region. This unrest was, no doubt, stimulated by the more extreme sections of the revolutionary elements, which the more moderate members of the local Workmen's and Soldiers' Council found great difficulty in keeping under control. Outwardly, however, Moscow and Petrograd, in spite of constant big demonstrations and meetings, were quite peaceful and orderly.

The Stockholm Conferences.

On our journey home we stayed at Stockholm, and held a conference with M. Branting, M. Huysmans, M. Van Kol, and M. Troelstra, all of whom we know well, on the subject of the proposed separate conferences between the various national Socialist majorities and minorities and the International Socialist Bureau Executive. They were exceedingly anxious that the British Socialist and Labour movement, both majority and minority, should come to Stockholm, and informed us that they hoped that the result of the conferences would be to place the responsibility for the war and its continuance upon Germany. They feared that unless England and France were represented the German influence would be very strong with the highly susceptible Russian Socialists. M. Branting and M. Van Kol are pro-Ally, but Troelstra is suspected of German sympathies. He informed me confidentially that he was responsible for the alteration in the policy of the German Foreign Office, which had at first refused to allow the German Socialist minority to go to Stockholm.

7

The Causes of the Revolution

While at Petrograd we endeavoured to discover the real causes of the revolution, and after consulting a number of persons of various political opinions we came to the conclusion that, although there had been much discontent in the army and among the civil population, together with considerable underground revolutionary propaganda prior to the outbreak, the downfall of the old régime was mainly due to a deliberate plan of the Government to provoke disturbances (which were to be suppressed) in order to justify further reactionary measures, and to bring about peace with Germany on the ground that Russia was not in a position, owing to internal troubles, to continue the war. This plan, however, failed because the soldiers who were expected to fire on the people refused, except in a few instances, to do so, and turned their arms against the authorities. We were assured that if the Tsar had consented a few weeks earlier to create a representative ministry with a moderate reform programme the revolution would not have taken place.

General Impressions.

We left Russia feeling that the leaders of the Workmen's and Soldiers' Council at Petrograd had at last felt the necessity of ceasing to be an Opposition Government, and were endeavouring conscientiously to co-operate with the Provisional Government to bring about order and stability in Russia. If Kerensky's energies hold out we think he will be the man to save the situation.

Conclusion.

In conclusion, we wish to place on record our appreciation of the kindness and attention which we received at the hands of His Majesty's Ambassadors at Petrograd, Christiania, and Stockholm, and of the British consuls at Moscow and Bergen.

W. S. SANDERS, Lieutenant.

o

APPENDIX III

EXCHANGE OF PRISONERS AGREEMENT

RUSSIA. No. 1 (1920).

AGREEMENT

BETWEEN

HIS MAJESTY'S GOVERNMENT AND THE SOVIET GOVERNMENT OF RUSSIA

FOR THE

EXCHANGE OF PRISONERS.

Presented to Parliament by Command of His Majesty.

LONDON:

PRINTED AND PUBLISHED BY
HIS MAJESTY'S STATIONERY OFFICE.

To be purchased through any Bookseller or directly from
H.M. STATIONERY OFFICE at the following addresses:
IMPERIAL HOUSE, KINGSWAY, LONDON, W.C. 2, and
28, ABINGDON STREET, LONDON, S.W. 1;
37, PETER STREET, MANCHESTER;
1, ST. ANDREW'S CRESCENT, CARDIFF;
23, FORTH STREET, EDINBURGH;
or from E. PONSONBY, LTD., 116, GRAFTON STREET, DUBLIN.

20

CONFIDENTIAL.

66

[201298]   No. 1.

Mr. O'Grady to Earl Curzon.—(Received July 5.)

Granville House, Arundel Street,
London, July 5, 1920.
My Lord,
I HAVE the honour to present to your Lordship the report of the work of the Delegation for the Exchange of Prisoners of War and Civilian Nationals with Soviet Russia, of which I was appointed head on the 15th November last.
I have, &c.
JAMES O'GRADY.

Enclosure.

British Delegation for the Exchange of Prisoners of War and Civilians with Soviet Russia.

REPORT.

ON the 13th November, 1919, I was appointed Chief of the British Delegation which His Majesty's Government proposed to send to Denmark in order to meet representatives of the Soviet Government.

The object of my mission was to attempt to secure the release and repatriation of all British prisoners of war in the hands of the Soviet Government, belonging to the navy, army and air force; to secure the repatriation to the United Kingdom of all British civilians, men, women and children, who were for various reasons prevented from leaving Russia though desirous of doing so ; to secure the release and repatriation of all British political prisoners undergoing sentences of imprisonment ; and to make such arrangements as were possible for the feeding, clothing and general welfare of such British subjects as might elect to remain in those parts of Russia governed by the Soviet. *Instructions.*

In order to achieve this object, I was empowered to attempt to exchange British prisoners of war in Russia for those Bolshevik prisoners of war in the hands of His Majesty's Government, a list of whose names was supplied to me.

In order to secure the release of British civilians, I was instructed to suggest the repatriation to Russia of such Russian subjects in the United Kingdom who might wish to return to their own country, and to inform the Soviet Government that His Majesty's Government were willing to make arrangements for the return to Soviet Russia of such Russian sympathisers of the Russian Government as were willing to be repatriated.

In accordance with these instructions I left London on the 15th November for Copenhagen to enter into negotiations with M. Litvinoff, the representative appointed by the Soviet Government to discuss with me the exchange of prisoners of war and civilian nationals between our respective Governments.

I arrived in Copenhagen on the 17th November, and was informed by His Britannic Majesty's Chargé d'Affaires that M. Litvinoff had been delayed, and was not expected to reach Copenhagen for some days. He arrived on Sunday, the 23rd November, accompanied by two lady secretaries, and the first meeting took place on Tuesday, the 25th November. *Meeting in Copenhagen.*

In accordance with my instructions I at once proceeded to call upon M. Litvinoff for a report on the health of all British subjects in Soviet Russia. M. Litvinoff replied that he had paid a visit to the British officers and men in Moscow prior to his departure for Copenhagen. He had heard there no complaints of ill-treatment, but complaints had been made regarding rations and the cold. This was not difficult to understand in view of the general shortage of food on the one hand, and the fact that the prisoners were ill-supplied with warm clothing on the other. At one time full liberty was given to all prisoners of war, and it was only when information reached the Soviet Government that Bolshevik prisoners in British hands were being maltreated that it was decided to restrict the liberty of the officers by way of reprisal. *Situation of British subjects in Russia. 1. Prisoners of war.*

318   [4519]   B

150

It is clear that M. Litvinoff could only have obtained this statement from sources favourable to the Bolshevik régime, and that it was therefore quite unauthentic. I at once refused to accept it, averring that, from my own knowledge, Russian prisoners in England were treated with every consideration, and indeed were in some degree in even better circumstances than many British labourers.

M. Litvinoff further stated that reprisals had taken place in the case of volunteers who took part in the Archangel expedition, who were interned in the Androievsky Monastery. In all other cases non-commissioned officers and men were provided with good accommodation, received rations, were at liberty to go where they liked, and were allowed to work for money if they desired. Their general welfare was looked after by Mr. North.

2. Civilians. As regards the British civilians, M. Litvinoff said he was aware of the suffering which attached to them, in common with the rest of the population, owing to shortage of food, provisions, &c. He pointed out, however, that foreigners in Soviet Russia had been subject to no special laws or regulations. Even after intervention had begun, no special measures had been taken against British and Allied subjects, with the exception of the arrest of diplomatic representatives in connection with his own arrest in London. A plot, however, was discovered on the occasion of General Yudenich's attack on Petrograd in June 1919, and documents of an incriminating character were found in certain foreign Legations. As a result of this, the Soviet Government began to institute measures of reprisal against foreigners, and certain British subjects were **Internment of certain British subjects.** interned. Some of these had, however, been released by his own intervention. Others, who were able to secure five citizens to testify their confidence in them, were not interned at all, whilst others were released after a short confinement. He thought that the number interned on his departure from Russia was not more than from ten to twenty.

Proposed principles of exchange. A discussion as to the principles upon which an exchange might be effected then took place, and M. Litvinoff at first proposed a partial exchange of military and civilian prisoners on a basis of the respective values of the prisoners to their Government. In making this proposal, he referred to the exchange of the Russian Commissar Raskolnikoff for the Goldsmith Mission. I informed M. Litvinoff that I could not entertain a proposal of this character. He thereupon proceeded to outline his proposals for a general exchange. In doing so he removed the scope of the negotiations far beyond their original object, arising out of the previous telegraphic correspondence between the British and Soviet Governments. He made demands involving :—

M. Litvinoff's proposals for general exchange.
1. The repatriation of Russian prisoners of war taken by the Allied and White Russian forces in Northern Russia during the period in which military operations were directed by the British staff.
2. Repatriation of Russian nationals residing or detained in neutral countries and desiring to return to Soviet Russia.
3. Reparation of Russian prisoners of war in Germany and Austria.
4. Reparation of Russian Soviet prisoners taken in the Caucasus and Persia and conveyed to India.
5. The appointment of Soviet representatives in neutral countries to supervise the repatriation of Russian nationals.

I at once informed M. Litvinoff that I could not discuss demands which bore no reference to the object of the negotiations and proceeded to put forward the following alternative proposals :—

Mr. O'Grady's alternative proposals.
1. All British subjects, military and civilian, in the hands of the Soviet Government, to be released.
2. All Russian prisoners and civilians, available for immediate exchange, to be released forthwith by the British Government.
3. His Majesty's Government to give certain guarantees to remove all obstacles, occasioned by the blockade and war, which might hinder the repatriation of Russian subjects in Great Britain, as soon as and when transport arrangements have been made, the form of such guarantees to be agreed upon by the Conference.

M. Litvinoff rejected these proposals : he objected to my omission of his clause 5, providing for the appointment of representatives of the Soviet Government abroad, and stated that it was essential that he, or someone else appointed for the purpose by his Government, should remain in Western Europe until the terms of any agreement which might be arrived at had been carried into effect. He further would not agree to the substitution of Great Britain for Europe and the other countries mentioned by him. He intimated, however, that he was open to discuss further suggestions. On the 5th December I therefore advanced the following proposals. In so doing, I informed M. Litvinoff that I was exceeding my instructions and that, although I was prepared to assume responsibility of referring them to my Government, he must clearly understand that they represented the maximum concessions which I felt myself at liberty to make.

1. The immediate exchange of all Russian prisoners of war within the jurisdiction of the British Government against all British prisoners of war in Soviet Russia. Mr. O'Grady's new proposals.

2. Repatriation by the British Government of all Russians in the United Kingdom who desire to return to Soviet Russia.

3. Repatriation of Russians taken prisoners in the Caucasus, on the Caspian and in Persia.

4. The British Government to make representations to the Government of Archangel with a view to the repatriation of all Soviet prisoners of war taken during the period of General Ironside's command of the forces operating against the Soviet army, as enumerated in the list supplied by the Soviet Government.

5. His Majesty's Government to approach the Governments of Denmark, Holland, Belgium and Switzerland with a view to the repatriation of all Russians interned in those countries.

M. Litvinoff summarily rejected these proposals, and subsequently reverted to his initial suggestion of a partial exchange, offering to exchange non-commissioned officers and men to the exclusion of officers.

On the 6th December, therefore, I referred to His Majesty's Government my original proposals and those advanced by M. Litvinoff in the course of the negotiations. Mr. O'Grady refers to His Majesty's Government.

His Majesty's Government replied that careful consideration had been given to M. Litvinoff's proposals and they had been found unreasonable. They included three points which His Majesty's Government were unable to entertain :— Reply of His Majesty's Government.

1. The suggestion that non-commissioned officers and men should be exchanged to the exclusion of officers.

2. That Russians outside the jurisdiction of the British Government should be introduced into the negotiations.

3. The disproportion in numbers involved, suggesting the repatriation of about 100 British prisoners against at least 2,000 Russians.

It was therefore thought that the time had come to inform M. Litvinoff that unless he modified his proposals no basis for the conclusion of an agreement could be arrived at.

The terms of this telegram were conveyed to M. Litvinoff on the 15th December. He replied that he was unable to reconsider the original proposals which he had made and said that he would refer to his Government for instructions. M. Litvinoff refers to his Government.

On the 18th December M. Litvinoff communicated to me its reply from which it appeared that they declined to reconsider the principles of negotiation which he had previously stated. I then asked M. Litvinoff if he had anything further to add and he replied that there was nothing further to be done. He therefore broke off negotiations. It was, however, decided that another meeting should be held to conclude with M. Litvinoff the necessary arrangements for sending supplies of food and clothing to British prisoners of war and civilian nationals in Russia, for ensuring a monthly transmission of letters and parcels to and from Soviet Russia and of money, if possible, as set forth in Annex 2 to this report. Negotiations broken off.

On the same day M. Litvinoff gave to Reuter's correspondent an interview which was telegraphed to London. This statement appeared to involve a sensible modification of the attitude hitherto adopted by him. His Majesty's Government therefore instructed me to endeavour to resume negotiations and stated that they were prepared to regard as a basis for further discussion the following four points set forth by M. Litvinoff in his interview with Reuter :— M. Litvinoff's interview with Reuter.

1. That His Majesty's Government should approach the Government of Archangel regarding the release and repatriation of the 225 Soviet Russian prisoners of war captured in Northern Russia and indicated on the list supplied by M. Litvinoff ; and should further undertake to release the Soviet Russians taken prisoner in the Caucasus, on the Caspian and in Persia.

4

2. That His Majesty's Government should undertake to provide transport facilities for repatriating Russians desirous of returning to Soviet Russia from Denmark, Holland, Belgium and Switzerland.

3. That His Majesty's Government should endeavour to secure the presence of a Soviet representative upon the Inter-Allied Commission in Berlin for the repatriation of Russian prisoners of war in Germany.

4. That His Majesty's Government should arrange for a Soviet representative to remain in some neutral country until the agreement had been carried out.

I was successful in resuming negotiations on the 20th December, and returned to London on the 23rd to confer with His Majesty's Government. I left for Copenhagen on the 3rd January, 1920, and from that time the conclusion of an agreement became dependent on a satisfactory solution of the first and third points stated above.

Delay: Archangel prisoners and Inter-Allied Commission in Berlin.

It was not until the second week in January that I received information that General Miller, commanding the White Russian forces in North Russia, was prepared to meet the wishes of His Majesty's Government. As regards the Inter-Allied Commission in Germany, I was informed that its affairs were being wound up, and a fortnight later it became evident that the German Government would not consent to

Inter-Allied Commission.

the formation of an international commission in its place. The question of Soviet representation on such a commission therefore disappeared.

The length of the negotiations was thus protracted far beyond the period which had originally been contemplated. The delay in effecting the release and repatriation of the prisoners of war and civilians caused me grave anxiety, which was further

Lieutenant Bremner's report, 5th February.

increased by the disturbing reports from Lieutenant Bremner, who passed through Copenhagen in the first days of February. I therefore endeavoured to prepare with M. Litvinoff the draft of an agreement which I proposed to sign with him, subject to the solution of the Archangel question, should further delay prevent its early settlement.

Preliminary draft agreement sent to Foreign Office, 18th January.

I was able to send a preliminary draft of the proposed agreement to the Foreign Office by bag on the 18th January. This draft was subsequently revised. I was, however, prevented from signing, as M. Litvinoff desired to exclude from its provisions

British imprisoned for grave offences.

British subjects in prison for what he described as "grave offences." Negotiations were still in progress on this point when I received a telegram from the Foreign Office

Foreign Office telegram, received 29th January, asking to await further instructions.

on the 29th January asking me not to agree to the draft pending further instructions from His Majesty's Government. On the 6th and 8th February I received two further telegrams informing me that a despatch containing a draft agreement, which had received the approval of the Cabinet, was being sent to Copenhagen by H.M.S. "Whirlwind" and indicating the course I should pursue. H.M.S. "Whirlwind" arrived on the 9th February and I received the despatch. M. Litvinoff was made acquainted with the terms of the draft agreement which it contained on the evening of that day.

Agreement signed 12th ...ary, 1...

Three days later an Agreement for the Exchange of Prisoners of War between His Majesty's Government and the Russian Soviet Government was signed by myself and M. Litvinoff. The terms of this agreement have already been published as a White Paper, a copy of which is attached to this report.

It was not without great difficulty that M. Litvinoff was induced to sign. He made objection to :—

1. Inclusion of article 8, binding the Soviet Government to return to the Archangel Government all officers, doctors and military clerks of the 5th North Rifle Regiment and the 2nd Battalion of the Artillery Division captured on the Onega, who wished to return to North Russia.

2. The inclusion in the terms of the agreement of British subjects imprisoned for grave offences alleged to have been committed by them against the Soviet Government.

3. The inclusion of clause 9, providing for the carrying out of the provisions of articles 1, 2, 3 and 7 immediately after the signing of the agreement, notwithstanding any delay which might take place before the putting into force of the arrangements contemplated in articles 4, 5, 6 and 8.

I declined to sign the agreement without the inclusion of points (1) and (2). To the inclusion of (1) he at last agreed. On the omission of point (2) he was, however, obdurate. It was, therefore only my desire to release from further suffering, under

Grave offences: Annex to agreement.

conditions which I had reason to believe had become intolerable, our prisoners of war and the great majority of our civilians, that I finally consented to a compromise whereby the release and repatriation of those in prison for grave offences was to

5

become the subject of further negotiation. I also agreed to the substitution for clause 9 of an annex in which M. Litvinoff and myself undertook to urge our respective Governments to carry the agreement into effect immediately.

As one of the four points forming a basis for the resumption of negotiations on the 19th December, His Majesty's Government agreed to endeavour to arrange for the residence of a Soviet representative in some country of Western Europe until the repatriation of Russians under the agreement had been effected. A clause to this effect, therefore, became the concluding article—No. 9—of the agreement. *Residence of Soviet Government representative in Europe.*

During the course of the discussions M. Litvinoff was under the impression that Great Britain exercised paramount authority throughout the world, and was therefore in a position to satisfy the demands he might put forward. I pointed out that this was not the case, and that the British Government could not dictate to other Governments what they should do. The utmost which His Majesty's Government could do to secure the repatriation of Russians interned in neutral countries was to represent to the Governments concerned the desirability of their being allowed to return to their own country and the readiness of His Majesty's Government to provide sea transport for their conveyance to a Baltic port, and to assure their unhindered passage from there to the Russian frontier. After many conversations I was successful in prevailing upon M. Litvinoff to recognise this. His Majesty's Government were subsequently successful in making arrangements with the Governments of Denmark, Holland, Belgium and Switzerland for the repatriation of Russians detained in those countries.

The enquiries which it became necessary for M. Litvinoff and myself to address to our respective Governments regarding the welfare of British and Russian subjects were attended with considerable delays, to be attributed in many cases to the remote areas in which the subjects of these enquiries were believed to be. In the case of enquiries instituted by M. Litvinoff, the frequent breakdown of the Lyngby Wireless Station in Denmark and a breakdown of the Petrograd and Moscow wireless stations caused delay in the transmission of messages, and the disorganised administration and transport in Russia itself sufficiently explains the long periods which elapsed before replies were received. On the other hand, the enquiries made by the Soviet Government necessitated investigations in India, Egypt, Australia, Archangel and South Russia.

The initiation of pourparlers between myself and M. Litvinoff at Copenhagen was the occasion of a campaign in the European press suggesting that the humanitarian mission with which I had been charged was only intended to cloak negotiations of a political character, and had as its ulterior purpose the recognition of the Soviet Government. I was therefore under the necessity of emphasising clearly that these suggestions were entirely devoid of any foundation in fact. Nevertheless, the widening of the scope of the pourparlers to include Russians in various parts of Europe and in Asia, the requests made by foreign Governments that I should negotiate for the release of their nationals, every request receiving willing assent of His Majesty's Government, and the relaxation of the blockade, made necessary by sending supplies of food, warm clothing and medicaments to British and foreign subjects in Russia, tended to confer upon the delegation an international character and to involve it in questions, like that of the blockade, which had been the subject of decisions taken by the Supreme Council of the Allied and Associated Powers. It thus became difficult to dissociate the negotiations from questions of an economic and political character remote from the immediate object of my mission. But on the whole I am of opinion that I was successful in so doing.

Up to the time of writing this report 124 British prisoners of war and 727 British nationals have been repatriated. There remain in Russia 16 British officers and men captured in Siberia, and whose repatriation is provided for under article 7 of the agreement; certain British subjects in prison for grave offences alleged to have been committed by them, and whom it was found impossible to include within the terms of the agreement; Mr. Keeling and Mr. Rayner were also in prison for what could not, in my judgment, be regarded as grave offences, and on behalf of whose release M. Litvinoff made urgent representations. They have now been permitted to leave Russia. There are also some 200 other British civilian nationals, who either do not desire to leave or who, for one reason or another, have hitherto been unable to do so. M. Litvinoff asked the Soviet Government to give all such British subjects who have not yet left Russia an opportunity of doing so, should they desire it, as occasion may offer.

6

I have to express my regret that the Soviet Government has declined to include within the terms of the agreement, or subsequently to release, those few British subjects who have been imprisoned for alleged grave offences. This regret is deepened by the knowledge that three of those detained are women, that there is reason to believe the conditions under which they are incarcerated to be harsh in the extreme, and that one at least of them is said to have been very ill.

Finally, I cannot conclude this report without stating my appreciation of the services rendered to me in my mission by Mr. (now Sir Robert) Nathan, who was with me for two of the four months of the negotiations; also the services of Mr. L. Gall, secretary to the mission, who undertook the work of Sir Robert Nathan when he returned to England, as well as his own onerous secretarial work; also the services of Mr. M. M. Cousins, of the War Office, performed with untiring zeal and energy as shorthand writer to the mission.

JAMES O'GRADY.

June 28, 1920.

Annex No. 1.

Routes taken by those Repatriated.

It was decided that the British prisoners of war and civilian subjects should return from Russia across the Finnish frontier. The existence of a quarantine station at Rajaojoki, on the frontier, where the disinfection of all persons leaving Russia took place, and the comparative efficiency of railway transport in Finland governed the choice of this route.

It was found impossible to accede to M. Litvinoff's desire that repatriation of Russians should take place through Esthonia, as the British Admiralty were unable to allow His Majesty's transport "Dongola" and the steamship "Tagus" to enter the port of Reval, at first owing to the ice conditions, and later owing to danger from mines when the ice broke up. The Dutch steamer "Lingestroom," however, proceeded with the Russians from Holland to Reval direct. The existence of a state of war between Finland and Russia made the Finnish route impracticable, and it was finally decided that repatriation of the Russians from the United Kingdom, Denmark and Switzerland should take place through Latvia, where the Lettish Government were contemplating the conclusion of an armistice with the Soviet Government. Arrangements were therefore made for the Russians to be disembarked at Libau, and Mr. Tallents, His Britannic Majesty's Commissioner for the Baltic Provinces, co-operated with the Lettish authorities in arranging for their transport by rail from Libau to the Lettish frontier.

Annex No. 2.

Supply of British Prisoners of War and Civilian Nationals in Russia with Food, Clothing and Medicaments.

Prior to his departure for London on the 23rd December, 1919, Mr. O'Grady concluded with M. Litvinoff an agreement for sending food, clothing and medical comforts to British prisoners of war and civilians in Russia, in return for which M. Litvinoff was allowed to send to Russia an equivalent weight of drugs for the use of the Soviet Government. This agreement became known as the "Ton for Ton Agreement."

Ton for ton agreement.

M. Litvinoff originally desired to make a purchase of 350 tons of drugs for the use of the Soviet Government. To assist him in making payment for these drugs, His Majesty's Government consented to allow the London branch of the Moscow-Narodny Bank to accept a deposit in London by the Soviet Government of Chinese Gold Reorganisation Loan, 1913, bonds to the approximate value of 150,000*l.*, for the purpose of effecting a preliminary purchase. M. Bubnov, the manager of the London branch of the bank, concluded with M. Litvinoff on the occasion of a visit to Copenhagen, the arrangements connected with the deposit of these securities.

M. Litvinoff desires to purchase drugs.

As, however, it was desirable that the necessities of British subjects in Russia should be relieved immediately, and as M. Litvinoff was unable to purchase within a short time more than a few tons of drugs, it was decided to allow him to complete his consignments with supplies of axes, agricultural machinery and piping, owned by the

First consignment: arrangements for despatch.

Soviet Government in Sweden and Germany. It became necessary to obtain the consent of the Swedish Government to the export of the axes from Sweden, in return for which permission, the Swedes were allowed to send 1 ton of supplies to Russia as part of our first consignment, for the relief of Swedish subjects in that country. The Danes were also given facilities to send a ton of food and clothing for their nationals in Russia.

In view of the uncertainty of ice conditions at Reval and of the unsatisfactory state of the Lettish–Russian frontier, it was decided to make arrangements for the despatch of consignments through Finland viâ Petrograd to Moscow. His Majesty's Government were successful in obtaining from the Finnish Government the necessary permission for this purpose and the Finns were enabled to send 1 ton of supplies for the relief of their compatriots in Soviet Russia. Further permission was subsequently obtained for the transport of a second consignment through Finland.

It was arranged that the freight costs for transporting both consignments as far as the Finnish frontier should be borne by His Majesty's Government and from the Russian frontier to Moscow by the Soviet Government.

As, moreover, M. Litvinoff refused to ask permission for the Rev. Mr. North to proceed to Petrograd to superintend distribution there, and no other satisfactory means of distribution in that city could be devised, I was reluctantly compelled to restrict the first consignment to the relief of the British colony in Moscow. Dr. Martiny was charged with the distribution of food and clothing in Petrograd when he subsequently accompanied the second consignment into Russia.

I was unsuccessful in endeavours which I made to induce M. Litvinoff to allow a British representative to accompany the consignments to Moscow and there assist the Rev. Mr. North in their distribution. M. Litvinoff at last agreed, however, to allow Dr. Martiny, of the Danish Red Cross, whose name he proposed, to proceed with the consignments to Moscow. Unfortunately Dr. Martiny was not available to accompany the first consignment. It was therefore agreed that Mr. Emil Nielsen, a British subject, whose services were lent for the purpose by the courtesy of Sir Charles Marling, the president of the Slesvig Commission, should take the first consignment to the Finnish frontier. They were there handed over by Mr. Nielsen to M. Eigtved, a representative of the Danish Red Cross, who had remained in Moscow, and was allowed to come to the frontier for the purpose of receiving and accompanying them to Moscow. (The Soviet consignment was handed over by Mr. Nielsen to the Soviet representative, M. Fineberg, at the same time. Receipts for both consignments were obtained.)

M. Litvinoff telegraphed to his Government asking that every effort should be made by the Soviet authorities to ensure the safe arrival of the consignment and to give every assistance to Mr. North in his task of distributing it.

It was subsequently ascertained from British prisoners of war on their release from Russia that Mr. North had received the supplies and had been helped in their distribution by naval and military prisoners. *Supplies received in Moscow.*

It was later found possible to extend the scope of the ton-for-ton agreement to include any other countries desiring to send food and clothing to their subjects remaining in Soviet Russia. In this way arrangements were made for the French to send 5 tons, and smaller quantities were sent by the Italians, Dutch, Serbians and Greeks. Further consignments were also sent by the Danes, Swedes and Finns. *Foreign consignments.*

On the 5th March Dr. Martiny left Copenhagen, and on the 19th March crossed the Finnish frontier with the second consignment of 17 tons and a similar consignment addressed to the Soviet Government. The consignment therefore reached Moscow in time for distribution before the second party of British prisoners of war and civilians left Russia on the 3rd April. *Dr. Martiny takes second consignment to Moscow.*

In view of the repatriation of the great majority of British subjects in Russia, it became unnecessary to send any further supplies for the purpose of their relief.

Annex No. 3.

Repatriation of Radek.

At an early stage of the negotiations M. Litvinoff informed me that Karl Radek, the Russian Bolshevik, who was formerly imprisoned in Germany, had been released and was preparing to return to Soviet Russia. As Radek had been appointed to participate in the conference being held at Dorpat between the Esthonian and Soviet

8

Governments, M. Litvinoff desired that he should be allowed to travel thither viâ Copenhagen, in which case he wished to have an opportunity of conversing with Radek on the occasion of his passing through Denmark. Should His Majesty's Government succeed in obtaining permission for him to pass through Denmark and undertake to convey him from Copenhagen to Reval, M. Litvinoff agreed to release two British officers and two other ranks, preference to be given to those in need of medical attention.

The Danish Government consented to allow Radek to pass through Copenhagen provided that he proceeded direct from the railway station on board a British war vessel and His Majesty's Government agreed to provide sea transport for him from Copenhagen to Reval. Unfortunately, however, the Spartacist rising in Berlin caused a dislocation of the telegraph service, and a telegram from M. Litvinoff to Radek, informing him that the Danish consul in Berlin would visa his passport on application, was not delivered. It was subsequently found that Radek had returned to Russia viâ Poland.

Notwithstanding the impossibility of carrying out the arrangements contemplated, M. Litvinoff requested the Soviet Government to release Lieutenant Bremner and three other ranks. As a result this officer, together with Corporal England and Privates Lambert and Sylvester, were released on the 28th January, 1920, and crossed the Finnish frontier two days later.

Marginal notes: Radek: To travel from Berlin to Dorpat viâ Copenhagen. / Spartacist rising: Radek fails to receive telegram. / Radek returns to Russia viâ Poland. / Notwithstanding, four prisoners of war released.

Annex No. 5.

Execution of the Agreement.

Part I.—REPATRIATION OF BRITISH.

On my arrival in Copenhagen, I received a letter from Sir Arthur Stanley, Chairman of the British Red Cross in London, intimating that the Copenhagen Bureau of the British Red Cross had been instructed to place their organisation at the disposal of the delegation in connection with such measures as it might become necessary to take for the relief and repatriation of our prisoners of war and civilian nationals in Russia.

Lady Marling, the President of the Copenhagen Bureau, and Sir (then Mr.) Martin Abrahamson, the Vice-President, were therefore entrusted with the purchase, assembling and despatch of supplies to British subjects in Russia, and subsequently with establishing a British repatriation organisation on the Finnish frontier.

On the 3rd March Lady Marling left Copenhagen for Finland to supervise arrangements for the reception of the returning British. She was preceded by Sir Martin Abrahamson, who made the preliminary arrangements at Terijoki, a short distance from the frontier station of Rajaojoki.

Lord Acton, His Britannic Majesty's Minister at Helsingfors, who had secured the co-operation of the Finnish authorities with a view to facilitating the transit of our supplies across Finland to Russia, approached the Finnish Government for the more comprehensive purpose of providing for the establishment of the repatriation organisation at the frontier. Lord Acton associated himself intimately with the work throughout, and when it was found possible for the British parties to pass through Helsingfors, he and Lady Acton extended a hearty welcome to and entertained them.

A due appreciation of the services rendered by the Finnish authorities—and of especially General Enckel, Chief of the General Staff, Colonel Bonsdorff, the officer commanding at the frontier station of Rajaojoki, Lieutenant Hongisto, and Dr. Gréal of the quarantine station—can only be made if it is remembered that a state of exists between Finland and Soviet Russia. Their help, therefore, in arranging for passage through Finland from Russia of several hundreds of persons, involved relaxation of many restrictions which military exigencies had imposed.

Terijoki was formerly a fashionable summer resort of wealthy Russian Petrograd. Thirteen empty villas were taken over and adapted for the accommodation of the refugees, Lady Marling taking up her headquarters at the Villa Salko.

The first party of British subjects to be released under the terms of the agreement came from Petrograd; they numbered 125 civilians and crossed the frontier on 10th March. On the following day another party arrived from Moscow, consisting of prisoners of war (1 officer and non-commissioned officers and men) and 184 ci On the 30th March two other parties reached Terijoki from Petrograd and l respectively. Fourteen prisoners of war (11 officers and 3 men) and 258 civilians (89 from Petrograd and 169 from Moscow) were repatriated on this occasion. A fortnight later—on the 14th of April—a further party of 48 civilians from Petrograd crossed the frontier, and on the following day, 14 prisoners of war (officers) and 103 civilians from Moscow. This party included the Rev. Mr. North. On the 27th of April 9 civilians arrived from Petrograd, and this was the last party to cross the frontier before the organisation for repatriating British subjects from Russia was closed down. The health of those repatriated was generally satisfactory. They were all placed in quarantine for fourteen days before leaving for England.

The release of Lieutenant Bremner and Corporal England, and Privates Lambert and Sylvester, took place on the 28th January, prior to the signing of the agreement, under circumstances which are related in Annex No. 4. Privates Harris and Parker were released subsequently, at the beginning of March, for reasons of health, and left Russia with Mr. George Lansbury.

There remain to be repatriated under the agreement the British officers and men captured in Siberia, and those British subjects who may for various reasons have been unable to leave Russia, as enumerated in pages 15 and 16 of the report.

Lady Marling worked with untiring energy. Disregarding considerations of health and the atmosphere of infectious illness in which the work was carried on, she ministered to the necessities of 845 British subjects on their leaving Russia after many months of privation and suffering. The volume of their gratitude stands in far more appropriate relation to all she accomplished than any tribute which I can pay. I desire, however, to add to this my own imperfect tribute and to acknowledge the loyal co-operation of Lady Marling and Sir Martin Abrahamson in the delegation's work. To its successful fruition they both contributed in a conspicuous degree.

I also wish to acknowledge the help which Sir Arthur Stanley and Mr. (now Sir P.) Agnew, of the British Red Cross, rendered in placing at my disposal a large quantity of stores for the relief of British subjects in Russia.

Part II.—REPATRIATION OF RUSSIANS.   and   and

On the 10th March the steamship "Tagus" arrived at Copenhagen for the purpose of conveying to Libau the escaped Russian prisoners of war in Denmark. These Russians numbered 2,300. As the steamship "Tagus" was only able to embark 1,200 persons at a time, it was necessary for her to return from Libau on completion of her first voyage and embark the remaining Russians, and take them to the same port. M. Litvinoff was allowed to proceed on board the "Tagus" to converse with his fellow-countrymen and he expressed himself completely satisfied with the accommodation provided for them. He was kept fully informed about all arrangements made and was thus enabled to advise his Government regarding the arrival of the Russians at the Lettish frontier, so that preparation could be made for their reception by the Soviet authorities. The arrangements for embarking the Russians in Denmark on board the "Tagus" were made by the Danish Government, assisted by His Britannic Majesty's Chargé d'Affaires at Copenhagen, the British Vice-Consul, Mr. Gall and M. Buchholz, a Red Cross representative of the Soviet Government, who always acted as intermediary between the Russian prisoners and the Danish Government.

Captain Hannam, of the "Tagus," reported that the Russians gave no trouble on board. Immediately on the embarkation of the first party, the President of the Russian Prisoners' Soviet asked the British Consul to convey to His Majesty's Government the gratitude of the prisoners at being enabled to return to their own country, and at the arrangements made for their accommodation on the "Tagus."

The steamship "Dongola" called at Copenhagen on the 23rd March, having on board the Russian prisoners of war from England. She conveyed these to Libau, subsequently proceeding to Finland, and returning to England with a party of British subjects repatriated from Russia. She then proceeded to Rotterdam and embarked a number of Russians from Switzerland, who were taken to Libau. Later, she again sailed to Finland, and brought back to England the remaining British prisoners of war and civilian nationals who had been allowed to leave Russia under the agreement.

On the 24th of April, the steamship "Lingestroom," a Dutch vessel, arrived at Copenhagen with 214 Russians who were being repatriated from Holland. She also embarked a few Russian subjects from Denmark by the courtesy of the Dutch Government. All these people were taken to Reval, to be conveyed thence to Russia.

Russians from
P⁻ᴸᵛium,
a and
Egypt.

"White"
Russian
prisoners.

There remain, therefore, to be repatriated under the agreement Russians from Belgium, India, and Egypt.

Under article 8 of the agreement the Soviet Government undertook to return to the Archangel Government all officers, doctors, and military clerks of the 5th North Rifle Regiment and the 2nd Battalion of the Artillery Division, captured on the Onega, who desired to return to North Russia, including those persons whose names appeared on Annex B. of the agreement, in so far as they could be identified. The Archangel Government ceased to exist before it was possible to repatriate any of these prisoners of war and the Soviet Government subsequently declined to take any steps to release them on the ground that the Archangel Government no longer existed and that the territory under its jurisdiction had passed into the hands of the Soviet forces before the conclusion of the Treaty of Capitulation, which had been the subject of an exchange of telegrams between Lord Curzon and the Soviet Government. On 11th March, having received instructions from His Majesty's Government, Mr. Gall informed M. Litvinoff that the British Government were unable to accept the contention of the Soviet Government that the latter were released from their obligations under article 8 by the fact that the collapse of the North Russian Government automatically set at liberty the Soviet prisoners of war who were to have been exchanged for Colonel Mikhaieff and other "White" Russian officers, and that His Britannic Majesty's Government desired to point out that the Soviet Government had entered into a contract and the fact that fortuitous circumstances, which were unforeseen at the time the contract was made, had given the Soviet Government benefits which they were to derive under the contract, would not in civil affairs release them from the duty of fulfilling the obligation incurred by them. Mr. Gall intimated, further, that the ordinary laws of contract are used for the interpretation of international agreements, and on behalf of His Majesty's Government requested M. Litvinoff to urge his Government to reconsider their decision and to release Colonel Mikhaieff and other prisoners involved. No steps were, however, subsequently taken by the Soviet Government to carry out their obligations under the article in question.

From information received from British prisoners of war it appears that several of the officers mentioned in Annex B. were killed either in the action referred to on Lake Onega, or subsequent to their capture by the Soviet forces.

o

APPENDIX IV

LIST OF BRITISH PRISONERS

LIST OF NAMES OF WAR PRISONERS IN RUSSIA.

No.	Name	Rank	Unit
1.	Frank Bruddle	pte.	Royal Army, Medical Corps
2.	Harry Wall	"	D.Coy. 45 Royal Fuseliers
3.	John Wynne	"	45 " "
4.	Frederick Swindon	"	45 " "
5.	Sydney Walter Bras	"	B.Coy. 45 " "
6.	William Needles	Lieutenant	Coldstream Guards
7.	John Ashton	pte	155 Hd. Amt. R.A.M.C.
8.	Thomas Cochrane	"	R.A.M.C.
9.	Bernard Loyle	"	155 Field Ambulance R'A.M.C.
10.	Alfred England	"	45 Royal Fuseliers A. Coy.
11.	James Arthur Field	Corporal	Royal Engineers 250 Signal
12.	John Harvey	pte	R.A.M.C.
13.	George Hopkins	"	155 Field Ambulance R.A.M.C.
14.	Joseph Mack	"	45 Royal Fuselier A.Coy.
15.	Ernest James Preston	"	45 R.F.A. Coy.
16.	Percy Parker	"	45 Royal Fuseliers B. Coy.
17.	John William Rhodes	"	155 Field Ambulance, R.A.M.C.
18.	Mark Edward Searle	"	45 Royal Fuseliers A.Coy.
19.	Jesse Frederick Underwood	pte.	K.O.S.B. Att. O.K.F.E. Bucks
20.	Yewos Roberts	Lieutenant	R.Welsh Fuseliers
21.	Reginald Henry King	Captain	R.A.S.C.
22.	Eric Arthur Bolton	2-nd Lieutenant	R.E.
23.	Robert Norman Dodds	"	Royal Engineer
24.	Cyril Norman Corleth	lieutenant	Highland Light Infantry Att.
25.	George Harold Hay	Captain	Royal Scots
26.	Francis Blackwell	"	West Yorkshire Regiment
27.	Albert Charles Thorn	Major	Machine Gun Corps
28.	George Koupell	Captain	East Survey
29.	Richard John Andrews	Colonel	Welsh Regt.
30.	Michael Monachan	lieutenant	Rifle Brigade
31.	Cocas Pritto	Sergeant	Middlesex, 13 Batal.
32.	Benjamin Gehr		Interpreter Section
33.	Frank Carter		1st Batal. Oxford and Bucks C Coy
34.	John Thomas Clements		4th Devons.
35.	John Milwany	Sergeant	Royal Dublin Fuseliers
36.	Daniel Lynn	Sapper	Royal Engineers Signals
37.	James Smith	Corporal	Royal Army Service Corps
38.	Alfred George Andrews	Sapper	Royal Engineer Signal Section
39.	Michael Dillon		Royal Engineers Wireless Section
40.	Rufus Webright		Royal Engineer
41.	John Keneth Peacock	pte	Yorkshire Regiment
42.	Norman Furnis	Corporal	6 Batt. Yorkshire Regt.
43.	Harry Leonard Beasly	Sapper	Royal Engineers Signals
44.	Richard George Triggs	Subconductor	Army Ordnance Corps
45.	Edgar Thomas Golby	Lance Corpl	Royal Army Service Corps
46.	Robert Todd Watson	2nd class aircraft	Royal Air Force No.4 Squadron
47.	Edward Nelson Harris	Lance Corpl.	Royal Engineers Signals
48.	Gordon Leath	Sapper	Royal Engineers Signals
49.	John Lavison	pte.	6th York's Regt. A Coy, 2 Platoon B Coy.
50.	Percy Dawson	Corporal	
51.	William George Miller	Sergeant	R.A.M.C.
52.	Sydney Arthur Foster	Sapper	R.Eng. Sign. Section
53.	Alexander Stevenson Chapman	Sapper	
54.	Lionel Francis Hilliere	pte	Royal Air Force
55.	Clifford Pickard	pte	6th Yorks.
56.	Robert Dawson		2/10 Royal Scots, C. Coy
57.	Albert William Richards	pte	High Yorks Regt. A Coy
58.	George Todd	Driver	
59.	George Lansdawn	Lieutenant	Royal Air Force
60.	Harold Lenox Marshall	Lieutenant pilot	R.A.F.
61.	Albert Sweeting	pte	45 Royal Fusilier
62.	Harry Ingram		R.A.F. 22 Squadron
63.	Antony Mantle	2nd Lieutenant	R.A.F. " "
64.	Henry Edward Clayton	pte	252 Machine Gun Corps
65.	Thomas Dunmow	pte	17 Kings Liverpools Att.
66.	Thomas Stringfellow	"	13th Yorks A Coy
67.	George Gay		H.M.S. Attentive R.N.
68.	George Yest	stoker	2/10 Royal Scots C Coy
69.	Thomas Carr	pte.	12 Platoon C Coy. 2/10
70.	David Paterson		Army Service Corps
71.	Robert William Brassil	Driver	2/10 Royal Scots, C.Coy
72.	William John Roberts	pte	2/10 " "
73.	William Laing		2/10 " "

```
 "   —74.  James Lambert — pte.          — 17 Kings Liverpool Regt.
 "  —75.  William Dinwoodie — pte.           2/10 Royal Scots
 "  —76.  Kenneth Leonard Nollett Able Sergat   Royal Navy
 "  —77.  Albert Peter Tiele —pte.         2/10 Royal Scots D. Coy,16 Platoon
 "  —78.  James Robertson — o  "              "    "     "      "
 "  —79.  William Henry Holly — pte.       2/10        "     "     "   D. Coy.
 "  —80.  Alexander Yorkston —  "          2/10        "     "     "   C   "
 "  —81.  Charles Robert Young —  "        2/10        "     "     "   C   "
 "  —82.  Hugh Mac—Intosh o    "           2/10        "     "     "   C   "
     —83.  Francis Tattam — 2nd Lieutenant( )    Clope Squadron N.R.E.F.
 "  —84.  George Young Robertson — pte     Royal Scots C. Coy.
     —85.  John Bedford Wilson — Captain( )   Royal Engineer
     —86.  George Alexander — Sergeant      Royal Engineer, Signal Corps
     —87.  Henry George Lapham — Lance Corp. 2/10 Royal Scots, C. Coy.
     —88.  Peter Watt — pte.               2/10 Royal Scots
     —89.  Herbert Victor Vordt — pte      2/10 Royal Scots. C Coy.
     —90.  Henry Harry Rose o    "            "      "     "    "
     —91.  John McGaffney —  "                "      "     "    "
     —92.  George William Stanley o  "        "      "     "    "
     —93.  Kenneth James McIntosh o  "        "      "     "    "
     —94.  Alfred John Pardon o    "          Royal Scots
     —95.  Rodger Pennycook o      "          2/10 Royal Scots
     —96.  Alexander Dingwall o    "           "      "     "
     —97.  Harry Hendry o          "           "      "     "    D Coy
     —98.  Ernest Hooton —corporal             "      "     "    "
     —99.  Archibald Frost —     Seaman        Navy
     —100. Alexander Forsyth o                 2/10 Royal Scots
     —101. Van der Spey — Colonel ( )
     —102. Ernest Ambrose Clark — pte.         Royal Marine Light Infantry
     —103. Frederick Hamlet o       "          45 Royal Fusiliers C Coy
     —104. Ronald Sykes — lieutenant ( )       Royal Air Force
     —105. Edwin Turner — pte. o               46 Royal Fusiliers
     —106. William McPhee — sergeant           46 Bn Royal Fusiliers
     —107. F.W. Sixton — pte.                  Royal Re Fusiliers
     —108. Henry Farlow o  "                   46 Royal Fusiliers
     —109. John Trottes    "                   3rd West York Regt.
```

NAVAL PRISONERS OF WAR in the

ANDRONIEV MONASTERY.

```
         1  Lieutenant L.W.S. Napier, R.N. ( )
         2       "       W.H. Bremern R.N. ( )
         3  Sub—lieutenant C.C.A.Giddy  R.N. ( )
         4  Under motor Mechanic B. Reynish o
         5    "        "        "    W. Whyle o
         6    "        "        "    H. Dunkley o
         7  Stoker Petty Officer S. McVeigh o
         8  Able Seaman          H. Bowles o
         9    "      "           C. Harvey o
```

APPENDIX V

INTERNATIONAL FEDERATION OF TRADE UNIONS
HEADQUARTERS: HOLLAND ===== 61 VONDELSTRAAT, AMSTERDAM

Post Box 1065
Letter: _____
Nr. _____
(In reply please quote Letter and Number)

AMSTERDAM, 18th November 1921

Dear O'Grady,

I wish to inform you that you are hereby appointed head of the Russian Famine Relief Commission of the International Federation of Trade Unions and that you are authorised by the Council of the International Federation to proceed to Russia for the purpose of setting up and directing a relief organisation under the terms of the Agreement concluded on the 15th October, 1921, between the representatives of the International Federation and those of the Russian Famine Relief Commission of the All-Russian Central Executive Committee.

You are therefore " the specially authorised representative" of the International Federation of Trade Unions as mentioned in Clause 2 of the Agreement and you will establish in Petrograd the central offices of our Famine Relief Commission as mentioned also in the same clause.

I would draw your attention specially to the provisions in Clause 4, whereby the Russian Soviet Government agree to grant to yourself and the members of your staff, the same protection and the same personal rights as are accorded to the representatives of the American Relief Administration, the German Red Cross, the Nansen Relief organisation and other relief commissions working in Russia.

INTERNATIONAL FEDERATION OF TRADE UNIONS
HEADQUARTERS: HOLLAND ===== 61 VONDELSTRAAT, AMSTERDAM

Post Box 1065
Letter: _____
Nr. _____
(In reply please quote Letter and Number)

AMSTERDAM, 18th November 1921

This letter constitutes your official credentials from the International Federation of Trade Unions as their Commissioner in Russia for famine relief.

I am,

Yours sincerely,

Secretary,
International Federation of Trade Unions.

APPENDIX VI

326   THE PAGEANT OF THE YEARS

7

THE ROAD TO FAMINE

In Petrograd I met a man who saved eleven million Russians from death, and had very few thanks and no gratitude from the Soviet Government for this tremendous rescue.

It was Colonel Haskell, who was directing the work of the A.R.A. in Russia. He was a tall, lean, silent man of the soldierly type, and I came to have a great respect and admiration for him. Under him was a first rate staff of enthusiastic, efficient, and brave men—it needed courage to face typhus in the famine districts—who carried out this enormous work of relief under heavy handicaps, because transport had broken down in Russia and they had to organise everything from scratch.

It was with the colonel and some of his staff that Spray and I travelled to the Volga and were able to report upon the famine as eye-witnesses of its dreadfulness. Without their help and comradeship we could not have gone.

We went from Moscow to Kazan in a train which panted, slowed down, and stopped after every twenty miles or so. Before we had been in it long one of the coaches caught fire and had to be left behind. Among our travelling companions was a white-haired old gentleman with blue eyes and the complexion of a new born babe, and the spirit of a Christian knight, or even of a Christian saint, with a sense of humour. It was Governor Goodrich of Indiana who had come to make a report on the famine conditions to the American Government. All through our journey he lived entirely on bread and apples and seemed to thrive on that diet. With us also was a young American doctor and one day he spoke grave words to a group of us sitting in his carriage.

"The adventure ahead," he said, "is not without peril. You fellows ought to realise that. Some of us are going to die of typhus."

It was curious and tragic that he was the only one among us who died of typhus.

After four days in that train we came to Kazan which lay under a heavy mantle of snow. It was now the capital of the Tartar Republic—a province of Soviet Russia—and was at the head of the richest grain growing district of the Volga valley. Now there was no grain because it had been burnt in its seed time by a terrible drought, leaving the peasants without food because their reserves had been taken up to feed the Red Army.

With deep snow on its roofs and lying thick on the ground so that no passing footsteps sounded it was like a city in a Russian fairy tale. Here in the old Czarist days nobles had built villas and laid out fine gardens for their pleasure in summer months. Now those houses were filled with refugees from famine, dying of hunger and disease, and across the snow came small children, hand in hand, who had walked a long way from starving villages where their parents were already dead. Like frozen birds many of them died in the snow. There were forty homes here for abandoned or wandering children. I went into a number of them and they were all alike in general character. In big, bare, rooms the children were naked and huddled together like little monkeys for warmth. There was no other warmth as there was no fuel. Their clothes had been burnt because of the lice which spread typhus among them. There were no other clothes to replace their ragged old sheepskins and woollen garments. Often it was too late to check the epidemic of typhus and thousands died and now were dying.

We went into the hospitals and they were dreadful. Because there was no fuel the patients, stricken with typhus, dysentery, and all kinds of diseases, lay together in unventilated wards. Many of the beds had been burnt for fuel, and most of the inmates lay on bare boards. Those who had beds lay four together, two one way and two the other. There were no medicines, no anæsthetics, no soap, no dressings.

In one of these hospitals, where I went with the American doctor, the nurses came rushing at us like wild animals. They were crying and wailing, and were fierce in their clutchings at us. They were crying out for food. They were starving. Some of them had caught the fever and their faces were flushed. They were dying of the diseases they could not cure.

"This is very terrible," said the young American doctor. "There is nothing we can do about it now. Somehow we must get them food and medicine."

He was deeply distressed and I felt sick, and nearly vomited in the yard outside because of the stench and the awful misery.

But there was a good opera even in Kazan. We went to hear it one night, and afterwards when we returned to our billet which we shared with some of the Americans we heard voices coming across the snow. There was a bang at the door and about a dozen members of the opera company including the Persian *prima donna* who had played the part of Carmen, surged into our room. Could we spare them any food? They were all starving, they told us in French and German and broken English. Our American friends brought out some of their rations. I looked at Spray and he nodded. The time had come to sacrifice that enormous Dutch cheese which we had bought in Berlin. At the sight of it the Persian *prima donna* gave a cry and leapt at it. Others shared her enthusiasm. Nothing was left of it but a little bit of rind which I kept as a relic.